The
RECOVERY
HANDBOOK

Don't read this book
if you don't want to change!

I might not make you a
"people person",
but you can become someone
people don't mind being around,
as much as they do now!

KENT R GORDON

COPYRIGHT 2023 Gordon Book Press

ISBN: 9798861525268

THANKS AGAIN

Thank you to my faithful wife and partner, who showed me how to work hard, put in long hours, sit in one place and get things done, and find a ministry and care for people. Thank you for your patience and help in getting this to the public, and for waiting just a few more years for me to finish the house I started.

KENT R GORDON

CONTENTS

KENT R GORDON

INTRODUCTION

Woke warrior? You were going to go to war to change the world. That didn't happen. Your best efforts, by in large, failed to produce the outcomes you hoped for. Marching around, rioting, calling people names, and expecting or forcing everyone to adopt your view of how things should be, didn't work to well. Woke is broke, or at least it's less effective than you had hoped! Are you really that surprised?

What did change? You went to war and YOU came back broken. (That is what often happens, by-the-way.)

You changed. You became less tolerant. You are not as happy as you once were. You have lost friends and alienated the ones still trying to hang in there. There are a whole host of topics that are now difficult for you to discuss thanks to your present mind-set, and the dysfunctional, broken, relationships you have created. Simply said, your woke attitude, words, and behavior have made conversation, and any type of progress, difficult.

How ironic that your once "allegedly" noble fight against intolerance and racism created and fostered the division and hatred you hoped to eliminate.

It's really fairly easy to understand how that failure occurred. You went to war with the wrong attitude, the wrong weapons, and with the wrong strategy. You fought a fight that was doomed to be lost before it started. Your choice of weapons have been these, ridicule, shame, criticism, lecture, destruction, division, etc. etc. Not surprising that the weapons you used had either little effect, no effect, or the opposite effect!

The only positive return you got, from your mild hostility or out-right temper-tantrum's and destruction, was a feeling of camaraderie with other angry souls and, for the moment, a brief feeling of nobility and some temporary sense of significance. Given the poor results, most of that is dissipating fast too.

You are now, understandably, tired, discouraged, and out of gas. You are not sure what to try next. You are out of ammunition. (To keep the "going-to-war" theme in-tact). Woke-ness betrayed you and set you adrift. (More about woke-ness just below.)

If you are open and honest, and/or if any of what I just said rings-true, then you are a person who can benefit from this book. Time for a fresh start? Time for a new you? Let's discover the new weapons and tools, and a new plan best suited to make the changes you know you need to make.

You need to pick the right battle this time, and the battle that may change everything is the battle to change who you are. Try that change next as that's a battle worth fighting!

This, from later in this book, "Discover the small, or perhaps large, change in perspective, thought, and attitude that will enable you to be the person you want to be with your spouse, your family, and among friends, associates, or employees. That really is the only place to start but that change in you may change everyone and everything else!"

Yes it seems, at least to me, that you can change things (yourself and others) after all! You just need to discover what works, re-organize, commit, and give it a try. Enjoy this book. Be honest, open, and introspective, and re-organize yourself the best you can.

WOKE-NESS

Let me directly address this idea of woke-ness.

I am sure a social scientist can tell you how woke-ness came to be. I assume it had its "evolution" and that, to those paying attention, there was a start date or an initial stage or expression of it some years ago.

I guess I wasn't paying attention or reading the right papers or journals but it seems to me that woke-ness hit us fast and hard. It seemed to pounce. It came from nowhere (or so it seemed that way to me).

Assuming, for the moment, that woke-ness evolved, let's define a few terms.

EVOLUTION: A process of continuous change from a lower, simpler, or worse to a higher, more complex, or better state.

DE-EVOLUTION: The notion that species can revert to supposedly more primitive forms over time, and, cynics also use the term "devolution" to refer to the perceived increasing dominance of the stupid.

Those two definitions suggest that we trend either up, or down. I guess there may be a third option for us, one called 'maintaining the status quo', but, as I look around I don't see that one as a possibility. We have not maintained the intact family, credible religious institutions, a fair and equitable justice system, reliable sources of health information, nor have we maintained an honest, unbiased, balanced, and representative governance. I could go on but you get the point, we are in decline/De-Evolution.

Hard to believe that in the 21st century we are trending toward stupid!

The above described failures are local, regional, national, and global. They are, in many ways, a small sampling of the many types of failures we see all around us. Most of these problems are complicated and they are far beyond our ability to fully grasp and solve.

Never-the-less, many folks take up arms and attempt to solve some of the many various problems we identify. Woke-warriors use the tools described above, "ridicule, shame, criticism, lecture, destruction, division, etc. etc." but much like Don Quixote, they find their tools and methods wholly unsuited to the task, or any stated goal.

How did "being critical" become mainstream? How did finding fault in others become acceptable, righteous, necessary, and even expected? The answer, at least on the surface, is easy. **We repackaged intolerance and a critical spirit and called it "being woke".**

Woke-ism, as we are perhaps now beginning to see, is not the positive change in social, moral, consciousness many claim it is. That move toward woke-ness is not evolutionary (in the best sense of the word). It's a metamorphosis that is de-evolutionary.

Did the woke agenda, attitude, and strategy fail? Yes is did, and it does. Finding fault, hating, and stoking division and intolerance is about as dangerous and harmful as one might expect. If you didn't buy-into this observation/statement the first time, here it is again.

"How ironic that your once "allegedly" noble fight against intolerance and racism created and fostered the division and hatred you hoped to eliminate."

The cause's and frustration's that brought about woke-ness are significant and they are many. The failure of the woke agenda and the damage it has done and is doing, is significant as well. I have avoided any specific definition of Woke because Woke-ness, like a cancer, spreads and it takes many different forms (as all forms of intolerance tend to do). I think it is one of those words or ideas that we all use, but it's a little hard to define. Thankfully, we don't need to define woke and set about fixing it. We throw it out. We cut out the cancer.

WHAT TO DO NOW?

For most of us, keeping track of ourselves is a monumental task. No need to worry about every body else, but of course, as we discussed, that is exactly what we tend to do. Now we have a name for that overblown sense of responsibility and over-sight. It's called "being woke". You know, that place/attitude where we are quick to point out just how wrong or misguided the other guy is, (almost tripping over our feet in the process.)

Yes, it's hard to focus on the outward and look inward at the same time.

 That abundance of critical oversight we all have, when combined with a lack of humble insight, may be the reason why nothing has changed out there, and it may also be why we feel worse on the inside, or "within"!

It's why you have lost the war, and it's why you are hurt, angry, and frustrated.!

This book helps you think about what we have created (woke or not), and more importantly, it helps you look inward. That inward reality is what you have the greatest control over anyway, (at least we hope you do)! It's also what you need to change first.

This book narrows our focus and hits closer to home. That's key because the changes that are possible for you and me are always those that start within, or, closer to home. They are those very personal acts, emotions, thoughts, words, and deeds that only we ourselves are responsible for. They are the ones we hopefully have a bit of control over and, as we said above, that's really the only place to start.

CAN IT BE DONE?

How am I going to write a book looking at how

critical you are without sounding critical myself? Here's how. I'm just going to ask you questions. You fill in the blanks. You decide what to fix.

Yes, that's the process. I set a scene, or describe a scenario, then I ask a few questions. (I might make a few observation's too.) You then take a step a back, seek the clarity that introspection and honesty brings, and then you hopefully set about finding a better course of action and commit yourself to it.

You decide what's working (or not working) and where a change in perspective, attitude, or action may be best. A critical spirit might be replaced by grace. (That might be good for, and feel good to, you and others). Conversation might replace belligerent hostility. (That might tend to solve problems and find consensus).

So, remember this. Your course of action, and any change for the better, always starts first and proceeds from your heart and mind. That's what we work on first and if you are open, brave, and sincerely interested in personal change and better outcomes, then positive change (in your heart and mind) will occur.

This book had a different cover, and the introduction was slanted differently. I printed both intro's for your viewing pleasure. This newer introduction (the one you just read), and the old one below, both eventually pose, or posed, this important question.

Why is different difficult for you?

(We reframed this question for the woke crowd and asked it another way just above. We asked them how they became alienated? Why is conversation difficult? Have you become less tolerant? Are you not as happy as you once were? Have you lost friends?)

The problems, the questions, the underlying solutions, and the homework for all of us remains the same, even if the title and cover changes. So, enjoy the book and do your homework. You are now learning how to live with those who are different (and that includes just about everyone) AND you are also working on recovery from "Woke-ness". It's all good work, any-way you slice it!

INTRODUCTION (The older one.)

THE IMPORTANCE OF

UNDERSTANDING DIFFERENCE.

Tolerance is not the same as understanding. It's

better than intolerance but it is not what we should aim for. Real understanding (and wisdom) includes conjuring the will power and taking the time to listen to, consider, and discuss another point of view. It is in your best interest to learn to listen and discuss openly in case there may be any benefit gained from such an effort. That type of personal, sincere, deliberate, effort, makes communication and progress among individuals, businesses, and nations, possible.

That, of course, is an understatement. It may be more accurate to say that refusal to consider: 1. what others may bring to the table, 2. all possible solutions, and 3. how others feel, is a tragic mistake, and that intolerance promotes alienation, harm, and failure on many different levels.

(It's also how a person looses whatever "war" they think they need to battle!)

Of course, we all understand that on some level we are not all the same, but coming to understand and believe that this is ok, and even preferable, is something altogether different. If I may be so bold, and if this book exceeds my wildest expectation, you might conclude the following:

"Being different must be okay and if properly understood it is a welcome part of our technicolor life."

What a cook is able to make is determined by

the different ingredients he has available and what he chooses to use. When a cook puts together different, specific, ingredients, they produce, make, or bake, different things. Ingredients are not good or bad in and of themselves, but understanding them and putting them together properly makes all the difference in the world. Ingredients, who come together and cooperate, make for a nice cake.

For our purposes here, understanding, accepting, and learning to work with different ingredients (or people), can make all the difference in the world, and in your world too.

(How, for instance, would "comming together" and concensus be, as opposed to disagreement and alienation?)

Because we are not the same, it is a "given" that understanding, accepting, and learning to work with different ingredients/people will be necessary. If you are going live and accommodate gracefully (the first step in constructive relationships and "progress" toward a goal) you will first need to understand why you find acceptance, adjustment, or acquiescence difficult. What about another point of view is disturbing to you? How did you become so rigid in your thinking? Are you demanding and hard to live with? Why can't you find a way to work and play with others that will be more effective?

You can see that I am already providing questions

for you to consider. This book is fully committed to your transformaton and that will only happens when you ask youself the hard, difficult, questions. The ones that cause you to stop, look, and listen, and find alternatives.

We must discuss these questions now because our current state of affairs suggests that change for the better is necessary. Intolerance, political correctness run-amuck, and uneducated, diffuse, angst dominate and control the discussion. (I'll let those who are more political or historical than I run with that last sentence any direction they chose, when they feel inclined and have the time.)

My interest is focused on the inter-personal. My interest is in helping us, first as individuals, grow gracefully, navigate socially, show respect, and embrace diversity, challenge, and change.

GOOD NEWS

As you adjust, everything and everyone around you will change too. That is the exciting thing. We are different but we are interconnected. That means you can have an effect on your surroundings, relationships, family, co-workers, and perhaps on your spouse.

CHAPTER ONE

DIFFERENCE IS DETERMINISTIC.

Our **differences determine** that we must learn to adjust or adapt in order to function with purpose, meaning, success, and civility.

DEFINITIONS

Definition One

Determinism: the doctrine that all events, including human choices and decisions, have sufficient causes.

This doctrine can be restated as follows: We are "caused" to make, and we must make, choices and decisions regarding how to live with each other because we are different.

<u>Definition Two</u>

Determinism: the doctrine that all facts and events exemplify natural laws.

This doctrine can be restated as follows: Laws of human behavior (what we know to be true about human behavior and interaction) indicate that when two or more people come together there will be discord, and there will need to be some adjustment, count on it, it's a fact of life!

ONE & TWO

If we combine the two definitions above, we come to these conclusions:

1. When two or more people come together we will see conflict and misunderstanding if poor choices are made.

2. This difficulty with difference (or poor choices) will occur with some degree of regularity and for specific reasons that can be discovered and stated. (As natural laws.)

3. If it is true that adjustment will be necessary, and that some of this needed adjustment can be understood, then we have a reason for thinking about our difficulties with others, and a basis for learning how to make adjustment in our thinking and motives, and/or, in our minds and hearts.

4. The fact that we are different "determines", or at least strongly suggests, that we consider the following, "natural laws" and make adjustments. (See below.)

THE NATURAL LAWS

1. Two or more people who come together, for whatever reason, will have to make specific adjustments depending on who they are individually and corporately, and what they bring to the table. They will need to make choices regarding how to live and function together.

2. The need for adjustment is something we can or should foresee, and that necessary adjustment is an "occurrence" that we can count on. (Just talk to anyone who is married.)

3. Two people, or a group of people, who come together, each with specific similarities and differences, will accomplish different types of things. If you want to make a nuclear bomb, then the people that you need to gather together are very specific types of folks. Be sure to understand that those folks will not make a cake, they will make a bomb.

4. How they will struggle individually and together, and the difficulties they will have, is pre-determined to some degree as well. In some sense, what they make and how they work together is already determined by who they are when they arrive.

5. Within that specifically designated group there are different skills, temperaments, and attitudes. It is in fact necessary for some of them to think "outside

the box". This suggests that "being different", may at times be a good thing.

6. No matter how carefully you designate your group, there will be those near you who are quite a bit different than you are. Some adjustment is always necessary. (Other points I make later in the book are not quite so obvious.)

7. When you understand that everyone is different, then you understand that outcomes, failures, and successes will be varied and some folks will do better, and some will do worse, than others.

That understanding suggests that It will be necessary for you to extend grace, mercy, and forgiveness. Empathy and tolerance must be extended to others, to those who are different, and even to those who fail. (Hint, be careful what you label as success or failure. That is a decision, that if not properly made can lead to rejection of people, failure to see better ideas, destruction of cohesiveness, and misery.)

8. When you realize that you are unique, or that you have your own skill-set and limitations, you can then understand what is possible, and what is not possible, for you to do. You can set goals that are attainable, ones that fit with who you are. That tends to eliminate the possibility of "failure" on your part, or the tendency for you to feel "worse" about it all.

9. While not everything is predetermined, you can

begin to operate with the knowledge that your skills are over here, and not over there. "Wisdom" tells you when to stay in your lane.

An aside, if you will. "Success" for you could be understood to be, a) becoming who you were intended to be, b) having good relationships, and, 3) attaining meaning and purpose in what you do.

10. That type of success is not predetermined but it can be yours, and it can be yours regardless of the ingredients you initially have to work with. In fact, your success is best determined by understanding, accepting, and using the ingredients you have!

11. Success can be yours, and it will be and look different than everyone else's. That must be understood to be oaky with you. If you find some degree of personal success and satisfaction, you will be less threatened by those who are different. That makes you make more agreeable!

12. Your relationships are also determined by what you do not know and cannot do. How well you understand failure (what you or others didn't know, or can't do) determines how angry, frustrated, or content you will be when something or someone disappoints you.

13. When you understand that everyone will not perform as you would desire and meet your predetermined expectations, or change as you would

prefer, you will feel will less pressure to change others, and you will have more patience. We will talk about that in a minute.

14. What you come to understand about relationships, and the various perspectives you can take toward those who are different than you, determines how well those relationships work or function, and how satisfactory they are for all concerned. This is true of almost any relationship you can mention.

15. The success we have living with our differences determines our quality of life. <u>Success is up to you.</u>

16. The most difficult relationships are the ones that have the potential to change a great deal for the better.

17. The most difficult relationships are the ones that have the potential to change YOU a great deal, and for the better.

This book will continue to discover and discuss how you can make changes for the better. <u>You determine your future.</u>

SUMMARY

These natural laws suggest that every day you will have opportunities to improve or degrade the relationships you have. How you relate to others and how satisfactory those relationships are, is up to you. You set your agenda. You decide what is important. You manage your insecurities and work to control your temperament. You decide if people are a priority. You bring wisdom, grace, and understanding, or you bring pressure, promote discord, and find resistance.

Since it is a given that people are different, you and I will each have our own unique set of circumstances, conflicts, temperments, and peculiarities to solve, change, and/or live with. We can say that your struggle is determined by who you are, who you are married to, who you work with, and the types of relationships you are going to be involved in.

How you struggle, and what you struggle with, is determined by by what you bring to the table (your skill-set) and by the differences you find in others as you come to know and understand them. Your success with and in those relationships, and their included frustrations and failures, is up to you!

MORE GOOD NEWS

Can you increase in wisdom and understanding? Can your skill-set be improved upon? Yes, there is hope. Some of what you know and do can be improved upon, and some things (people and circumstances) might remain the same. It takes wisdom to know which is which, and wisdom to work on changing, or accepting and understanding, both.

<u>We must decide what to work on within, and what to accept and appreciate in those who are not like us. The fact that we are different demands that we do just that.</u>

How well you understand and apply *The WOKE RECOVERY HANDBOOK* will determine:

1) how pleasing and satisfactory your relationships are to you.

2) how meaningful your friendships and relationships will be with and for others as well.

On a very practical level, your understanding of differences will also,

3) determine how successful you will be.

You can learn how to, "be nice and play with others", and if you're careful, you can influence others to everyone's benefit.

The rest of the book is a discussion of what these differences are, how to be comfortable with the differences between people, how to accept the differences that cannot change, and, how to make adjustments in your thinking, your heart, and in your behavior.

Let's look at how you deal with those who are

different. Perhaps that is the only place to start. Let's make adjustments to your perspective, attitude, and to your skill-set.

A FEW NOTES ABOUT APPLICATION

This notion about the importance of understanding differences can be applied most everywhere. I will talk about marriage on occasion in this book because that is how this idea of accepting "difference" came to be part of my struggle, and eventually part of my understanding. I first applied these natural laws or observations in my relationship with my wife, but they go much further and they apply to many different relationships and circumstances. If an observation applies to your circumstance and that circumstance is different than the example I am using, that is fine.

This is how this concept of, and deeper understanding of, being different started for me. I have been married for 40 years. Most that time she and I have been working full time in different places. I have not needed or relied on her at work, and she has done just fine without me. In fact, what she does is so completely foreign to me that I could not have helped her if she asked, even though I might want to lend a hand. We each drove to completely different places and had different responsibilities and obligations, and that was just fine for 38 years.

Now we are retired and we are on vacation in the same car. Yes, that is quite a bit different and it takes some adjustment. In fact, it takes quite a bit of adjustment on both our parts. (It seems like the only adjustment that is happening at the moment is mine, at least that is how it seems to me. Don't be surprised if you feel that same way some or most of the time as you do the work this book suggests.)

To be fair and honest, Jan has made many adjustments and has probably been waiting patiently for 38 years for some adjustment on my part. If I think about it, my adjustment is the only adjustment I have any control over anyway! It is foolish and frustrating to expect everyone else, even the wife, to change first. Took me 38 years, and countng, to figure that one out!

Read that again, you and your adjustment may be a good starting point for you too. It may initially be the only change you can make, but, as you adjust, everything and everyone around you will change too. **That is the exciting thing. We are different but we are interconnected.** That means you can have an effect on your surroundings, relationships, family, co-workers, and perhaps on your spouse.

Back to the "always dangerous" spouse example. I have backpacked all over the Serra Nevada Mountains, and reading a map, topographical or not, is second nature. It never occurred to me that my wife could not read a map, or that the spinning arrow on a cell phone map would be indecipherable to her.

I know you can't tell what my feeling are about this at the moment so I'll just confess that am still having a bit of trouble with this difference between her and me. I must accept her as "different" and the degree to how well I successfully accomplish that task has ramifications for how well our relationship will work, and how happy she and I will be on this vacation and elsewhere. (It's a little late to find another navigator, nor would I want to.)

On a related note. It is possible to be happily married to someone who, at times, aggravates and frustrates you. This means that you must accept the fact that the relationship you two create will be of a particular kind, have a specific downside, and have difficulties and benefits that only come by being married to that particular person. Don't go through life disappointed that you, or the two of you, cannot make something different than what it is possible for you to make together. This, in essence, means that you will have to work with what you each bring to the marriage, and you will struggle in ways that are unique to, or determined by, your "mix of ingredients".

We often say something like this, "You each brought your own baggage to the relationship, and that is what you will have to deal with". By accepting this difference in experience, expectation, temperament, attitude, and style, you can have some degree of patience as you work out your differences. Be sure to understand that, "working out your differences", does not mean that you work to change the other person. It means adjustment on both your parts. It means that you accept the fact that you are different, then learn how to come together in-spite of, or because of, those differences.

I am not sure but that may be the end of the "marriage counseling" portion of this book, just in case you were wondering or worrying. I might actually throw in a couple more comments, but I won't over-do it.

In general, it can be said that If you want to improve relationships, of any type, you must gain insights and practice applying what you can, and, (as we will discuss) successful relationships, or even improvement in ones already established, are their own reward.

I have introduced a lot of topics and possible directions to go. As you read, begin the learning process like this:

1. Pay attention to those observations that are obviously true.

2. Why did that observation catch your attention?

3. Does the book always seem to be talking about someone else?

4. Is it always the other person who needs to change?

5. Are you offended that I suggest you have work to do?

6. Are you defensive?

7. Does that chapter or does that observation indicate a problem area for you?

8. What emotions and feelings are stirred up?

9. Does the chapter suggest something that you are convinced you are unable to do?

10. Do the observations suggest you might need to do a few things differently?

I could mention more keys to understanding and application, but you get the idea. Read the book, be open-minded, and be introspective first. Discover the small changes in perspective, thought, and attitude that will enable you to be the person you want to be with your spouse, in your family, and among your friends, associates, or employees. Remember, "That really is the only place you can start, but that change in you may change everyone and everything else!"

Let's keep going and you can do the application as you gain insight, and as seems best to you.

CAUTION

Don't let the short length of this book fool you. We are discussing major stuff here. I would guess that at least every other page brings something to seriously consider, a challenge for you, or a task that is monumental. Change at our/your core is difficult indeed. We are broken right out-of-the-chute, and most of what we learn or experience is probably not that helpful. (I guess that means that there is probably lots of room for improvement!)

1. This book asks you a lot of questions. That means there is ample opportunity for you to go deeper and understand yourself more fully, and then seek to make improvements.

2. There are many little hint's mixed in as to how you can manage your ego, your insecurities, and your temperament.

3. The book also suggests many changes in thought and perspective.

4. #1-3 taken together, or even one at a time, produce better outcomes.

You do want to, "gain friends and influence enemies" don't you ?

Here are a few more questions to help you go deeper.

Can you think of a relationship that needs a little work?

Do you owe someone an apology?

Are you in touch with your emotions?

Why do you react as you do?

Why do conversations go sideways?

Are you a member of a dysfunctional family?

Are you a member of a failed coup?

Can you improve your interpersonal skill set?

Don't freak-out!

I think that you and I can work on most of that.

Let's take a closer look!

KENT R GORDON

CHAPTER TWO

UNDERSTANDING DIFFERENCE
DECREASES PRESSURE.

1. <u>You don't have to know everything, or micro-manage everything.</u> Let's leave behind the idea or illustration of making a bomb, or baking a cake. Let's talk about building a car instead.

Your expertise may be in making electrical wiring harnesses. You understand how to interconnect the various electrical devices necessary to make the car run. You don't need to understand the cooling system. They, the folks tasked with that responsibility, do not need your 2 cents. They do not need to make a cooling system that conforms to rules and theories regarding electricity, capacitors, resistors, and regulators that govern the charging and ignition systems. They have their own rules and regulations, and frankly, you don't understand them too well!

The concept of "difference" suggests that others will do better in areas that are not your strong suit.

Your "skill set" suggests that you will do best in some other area. ("Mind your own damn business", is usually the way it is stated.) Can you think of a situation where you are "in over your head" or ill equipped to handle the problem?

You simply do not need to take on responsibility, (pressure), that you are ill prepared to have.

2. What makes you think that you are always right? If you think you are always right, or always have to be right, then we have bigger problems than I thought! (See "Bonus Thoughts" just below.)

You need not always impose your will or even your suggestions as that creates pressure on others. Step back. Is it possible that you have it wrong, or that another solution is better? Are there times when you seem to be on the outside looking in? Is that okay, or do you need to be at the center of, or manipulate, everything? Why do you feel threatened? Why are you insecure?

The self-inflicted pressure to be right and have everyone else agree, takes a tremendous toll on everyone.

3. It is not always necessary or even preferable that something is done as you would tend to do it.

When you do not labor under the impression that every idea you have needs to be heard and considered, you may discover that someone has a better idea than you.

You may discover that different is better, or at minimum (as we have discussed), you can learn that not everyone has to do it your way. That freedom of diversity and expression promotes communication and supports others. How can you change the culture for the better? How can you encourage diversity of thought, and how will that motivate those around you to participate and add to the whole? What progress can then be made?

When there is no pressure to always conform, and other ideas are tolerated and even considered, the differences can add to the whole.

4. You can and perhaps should, if not too cruel, allow others to fail or succeed, at least at times, on their own. The scientific method is in-part based on trial and error. Doing something different, or combining elements in an unusual way, is a necessary step in change, invention, and progress.

Proposing, testing, failure, and recovery create character, and, that failure/recovery cycle is part of the discovery and creativity process that benefits everyone.

What have you missed out on in your personal or corporate relationships because you were resistant, concerned about disapproval, and, afraid of challenge or change? How has the company fallen short, or what has it missed, because others were not included and listened to?

I will acknowledge that there are times when rules,

regulations, and procedures must be followed, but, a "heavy hand" used to force conformity is not always necessary, if needed at all. Perhaps you fancy yourself a boss, or actually are one. How do you get others to cooperate and "get on board"? What toll does your management style take on your employees, and on your mental health? Do employees respond to pressure, or encouragement?

The real interesting question may be this. Do some of them have a better idea, and would you even hear it if it were expressed?

<u>The point is that control and pressure kills creativity and creates a work space, or living space, that just does not need to exist.</u>

SUMMARY

Can you begin to see and understand that the difference between individuals does not call for pressure and conformity? It suggests just the opposite. Allowing for difference in expression, idea, and even attitude, can create an environment of anticipation, discovery, and growth. The pressure to conform and perform can be replaced by the incentive to share, explore, and be understood and valued. Diversity, challenge, discussion, acceptance, and change, are earmarks of a good company, relationship, or marriage.

BONUS THOUGHTS

Let me call for a little introspection on your part. (You should already be introspective. Goodness knows I've given you enough questions to get you started.)

Where is the pressure you feel, or the desire to impose your will on others, coming from? Are you threatened by those who are different? Is a challenge or threat to your supposed authority an unacceptable and frightening "thing"? Can someone be different than you and not throw your world out of balance? Is another persons' failure to conform to your wishes a cause for anger? Is there great pressure to keep things under control for fear of "losing it" completely?

<u>Perhaps your trouble is not with someone who is different. You have trouble with your feelings about who you are. Perhaps you are not really comfortable with who you are and how it is that you are different than, (read "less-than"), others.</u>

The real pressure you feel is the pressure you maintain and express due to unresolved conflict and insecurity. You feel the pressure of being found out and shown to be a fraud.

We will touch on these very personal problem areas in this book, and I will give you some alterntive thought's and persepctive's so you can "go deeper". Just be advised that the changes that you think are necessary probably start with you. We all struggle with who we are, and in that sense, you are not that much different than everyone else! Can't say it enough, Remember to, "Read the book, be open-minded, and be introspective first."

APPLICATION

I suggest this: If you spend as much time understanding who you are, how you think, what you feel, and how you act in your surroundings, as you do implementing and carrying out your will and pressuring others, you will find that relationships will improve.

The most important change may be the growth you see in yourself as you learn to be tolerant, and as you learn to listen to, and value, others.

That may change everything!

(Or at least take some of the pressure off!)

CHAPTER THREE

DIFFERENT DEMANDS ADJUSTMENT.

My wife and I were in Spain and she was trying to tell the waiter what she wanted for breakfast. There was communication difficulty between my wife and the waiter. I was using hand signals because I am not as smart as her. She was attempting to speak Spanish. They were having difficulty understanding and agreeing on the difference between tortilla, tostada, and toast. It was not his fault that he could not understand. He was just different, and he was not different due to some defect or lack of trying, he was just different than we were.

1. It is selfish and self-centered to assume and expect that others will rapidly and eagerly understand and accept your point of view, or change theirs. It might be said (and I can't believe I am saying this in print) that the "fault" was on my wife's side. I think I'll be safe and rephrase that, "The fault was on OUR side". We were in his country or "space", (as it is popular to say). The waiter was not stupid, belligerent, or hostile, he just didn't speak our language and <u>it was not his obligation to consider changing either who he was or how he communicated to us.</u>

2. If they, whoever they are, are different and have trouble understanding you then you are going to have to consider changing the way you communicate. Much of the time we think that the other person needs to make an adjustment. If the other person "should" consider a change, that is a change you may have trouble suggesting and enforcing anyway. Their adjustment, is a responsibility you don't have. <u>Don't pressure others to understand or change, make an adjustment in yourself first.</u>

3. When you enter someone else's "space" there is an implied obligation that you learn and attempt to express yourselves in a way that can be understood by them. We actually did manage to frustrate a few waiters but that was not our intent. "Intent", is somewhat irrelevant. <u>What is relevant, and what indeed may have been helpful, would have been for us to learn how to communicate more clearly with them before we arrived.</u>

Much of this book is aimed at preparing you for those times when you encounter those who are different. My intent is to help you see others in a different way, understand your areas of difficulty, adjust your perspective and attitude, then help you do what is best as you enter their "space". You can anticipate, prepare, and then change interactions and relationships for the better. I hope that is your intent too.

I shouldn't have to add this, but I think I must. <u>If person is entering "your space" your obligation is still the same. See others in a different way, understand your areas of difficulty, adjust your perspective and attitude, then do what is best.</u>

SUMMARY

Those who are different than you, and that includes just about everyone, will not automatically agree with you or even always understand what you are saying. There are a variety of reasons for this. They may not care to listen, or they may not understand when they do.

The obligation to make yourself understood is yours, and it will go better for you when you gain some understanding, patience, and skill in communication. <u>A personal, concentrated, effort, to change the way you communicate is a good option, and sometimes it is your only option if you want to have some degree of success in relationships, and with outcomes. That type of adjustment is yours to make.</u>

APPLICATION/OPTIONS

If someone doesn't understand you, how do you react? Are they more likely to respond better if you are patient? If you adjust what you say and how you say it, will you get better results? Pay close attention to your next difficult conversation and try to notice how it goes wrong and why. What did you expect, and was that reasonable? What can you do differently? Hint, try to catch, see, and understand or name those emotions that rise so quickly to the surface.

Try to understand what you are doing

and feeling,

before everything

goes sideways!

CHAPTER FOUR

DIFFERENT IS NOT "RUDENESS", ETC.

I want to emphasize again that a person who does not understand you may not be at fault. The waiter in Spain was not at fault, and he was not being rude when he had trouble understanding what we wanted for breakfast. He just had a different way of speaking. The words he used were not the same as the ones we were using. <u>That difference does not need to be labeled as either good or bad.</u>

It's okay that he is different. (Of course, he may have been rude too, but we couldn't understand that either.)

1. A relationship that is judgmental, labels another person, or includes acrimony is a relationship that needs attention.

2. When you categorize the other person as a problem, or the discussion as argumentative too quickly, you prejudge and you may, 1) mistake the other persons' motivation, and, 2) misunderstand the problem.

3. Your judgmental attitude, undeserved assumptions, and subsequent labeling, makes him or

her your foe or nemesis.

4. When you assign labels, to those who are different, when you say someone is "rude", or "not trying", or "not listening", you are deciding that there is a flaw in their character, and, that the problem is on their end.

5. The second you assume some fault in the other person you remove yourself from that frame of mind that seeks to solve the problem, whatever it is. Your quick or even "automatic decision" to place blame on the "rude" person in front of you tends to remove any responsibility from you. You start reacting, and fail to find solutions that truly help.

6. Your judgmental attitude "ices" the relationship and brings it to a stand-still. Your bad attitude stops the other person in their tracks. It discourages conversation and flexibility. They resist and shut down.

7. You next somehow give yourself permission to become impatient and intolerant. That makes you the rude person.

8. If a person just doesn't get it, there usually remains the opportunity for you to fine tune your presentation and improve the discussion. Cluelessness (both theirs and/or yours) is workable, but rudeness, especially yours, or not trying, makes everything more difficult.

APPLICATION

Exactly how did the relationship get to the point of rudeness, name calling, and resistance? (If you insist on labeling it.) Are you willing to "own" your part in the communication problem? Is it outside the realm of possibility for you to reconsider your assessment of the other person? Could it be that they are not rude, hostile, or indifferent, they are just different? They may be open to suggestion. <u>They may want to communicate but they are just having trouble with you and your attitude!</u>

Are there people in your life that you are unable to work with? Are they on a "different planet" or "out to lunch"? Some folks will admittedly be more of a challenge than others, but don't be quick to judge them or your relationship with them as somehow impossible. What if I suggest that it is possible for you to just view them as different? Find out how to communicate to each individual you run across. What type of feed-back are they open to? How do you best communicate with them?

Are you aware of why you had an adverse reaction to someone you just met? Do you maintain a certain stance, or place people in categories so that you can better manage them, gain an advantage, or keep them in check? Do you have words, nicknames, or labels for others? What labels are you wearing? What do people say about you?

AN OPTION

Let me try to tweak your perspective and attitude. Instead of saying, "they are frustrating" (a label) why not see them as frustrated. Don't label a person as "needy", ask instead, what do they need? Understand the individual, their frustrations, and how the relationship can be improved as that is the first step to finding a solution.

1. Use labels to accurately name what is going on in the relationship.

2. Use labels and descriptions to help define the problem, not to place blame and absolve yourself of responsibility.

3. Label or pick a point of view or attitude that you want to adopt. One that will make for a better outcome.

I didn't talk a lot about 1-8 just above. They are obvious and self-explanatory. What I do want to point out is that we go from one to eight in a split second. A conversation can turn on-a-dime and head for disaster. All these things (1-8) happen very fast, so you need to be on top of your game before you walk in the door. Makes no difference whether it is the door to the office, or the door at home. <u>You must endeavor to be the person you want to be. If you don't know what type of person you want to be, then you have work to do; no one else, just you!</u>

SUMMARY

Labeling any person or relationship, or distancing yourself and placing that relationship in a category that assumes it is difficult or impossible, is a losing proposition. Of course, if a person is having trouble understanding you it may be due to no fault of their own. If that is the case, then the problem is on your end. Could it be said that you are impatient, intolerant, smug, and somewhat oblivious to the circumstances and what may be necessary in order to communicate clearly? See if any of those labels in the last sentence fit you?

Look at your relationships and how they go wrong so you can make improvements and ease tensions. The responsibility is first and foremost yours. See what you can do to change the "dynamic". See if you can view and label others differently.

How hard are you going to work at the adjustments you need to make?

You may even need to learn Spanish!

I've been re-reading and editing and I am not sure that APPLICATION, SUMMARY, and OPTION are three distinct categories. At least not the way I am doing it.

Not sure I am supposed to raise a question at the last minute in a SUMMARY.

Am I supposed to ask questions in the APPLICATION section, or just tell you what to do?

I seem to have questions all over the place. Work with any question that seems to intrigue or challenge you, and especially any question that you wish wasn't there, even if I seem to have put it in the wrong place.

CHAPTER FIVE

DIFFERENT IS JUST DIFFERENT

Different is not necessarily wrong, it's just different. In fact, "different", may not really mean very much at all. I think I have talked about this one way or the other.

1. I just want to say here that it is not always necessary to attach labels or even feelings to thoughts, notions, and people who are different. It may serve no real purpose to do that. Different just may be different with no labels needed, eyebrows ruffled, or feelings attached.

2. A different opinion does not mean that "you are wrong",. There may be no need to "feel threatened", or need to attack another person. Let them be different.

3. You may be giving this alleged "difference problem" more credit than it deserves. The world may not end, the relationship may recover, you may not be reduced to a puddle on the ground.

4. Different may just be something that occurs on occasion and you may just a have to, "roll with it". A variation on another phrase would be this, "Different happens!"

SUMMARY

Relax, take a load off.

APPLICATION

Relax, take a load off.

"Roll with it"

"Different happens!"

(As you can see, I avoided question's in both the summary, and the application!)

CHAPTER SIX

DIFFERENCE IS NOT OK WITH YOU.

Okay, chapter 5 just wasn't your chapter. Relaxing is not an option, yet. You don't quite have the knack of, "rolling with it". You're not there yet. You get "bowled over". Feeling's get attached all the time, and to everyone.

You are still carrying a heavy load. You cannot let go, forgive, approach, or turn yourself around. Let's look at your mistakes in attutude, perspective, and judgement, and see the BIG downside.

1. If your emphasis is on the difference in others, <u>you will not find agreement and harmony.</u>

2. It may be that different is not okay with you because it leaves your position suspect and that is threatening to you on many different levels. <u>You will always be on guard.</u>

3. If your ego prompts, suggests, or drives you to change other people, then the problem is not the other person or their idea. <u>The problem is your ego.</u>

4. If you are insecure, or used to getting your own way, you will probably find it necessary that others validate you and your opinion. <u>You will never be</u>

satisfied.

5. When that effort to find agreement and validation fails you, you compensate by putting down others and dismissing their opinions. You will be alone.

6. The worst-case scenario is that your defensiveness drives you to fight for a position that is not as credible as the one you are fighting against. Yes, that is how distorted your vision is, and how convoluted your arguments can become when different is not ok. No one wins.

These strategies, or defensive postures, come from a stance that is built on quicksand. Your footing is suspect so you focus on others and require that they validate your opinion or change theirs. You are sensitive, and you must be secure. Your lack of ego requires it.

I must admit that the "ego problem" goes another direction. It may be that your ego is not super sensitive. It may be that your ego is so big that you are convinced that your position is the only one that is valid, and your position should be considered and adopted. Remember and understand that even a "good opinion" poorly presented, or insisted on, is difficult to accept. That, of course, means that your idea might be right, but your attitude get's in the way.

Also remember that the finding that your opinion is "righteous" (or right) is highly subjective.

SUMMARY

I think you're getting it by now. Aren't we all at times consumed or driven by ego, pride, self-preservation, the need to be right, and the need to be affirmed? What if WE looked at OUR insecurities, and addressed OUR fears and short-comings first?

How much better would it be if we understood our motives, kept ourselves in check, and held ourselves to a higher standard? What if we looked out for the interests of others, strived to be gracious and extended peace, instead of resistance and criticism? What if we treated others the way we want to be treated? Would our world be better? Would your world be better?

FALURE TO DO THIS prompts and promotes the enevitable consequences we listed at the start of this chapter (1-6). The downside is indeed grave.

Allowing and accepting disagreement is an indicator that you are mature and reasonable. It indicates that you are secure in who you are. A person who is "squared away" accepts disagreement as the natural and necessary course of events. You know that disagreement is inevitable, and disagreement may even be one necessary aspect of good, open, communication and compromise.

Find a way for disagreement and difference to be ok because, "different happens", and different adds to the whole.

APPLICATION

I am sure there are many sophisticated observations that can or should be made about the id, the ego, and superego. I'm not going to go there. What is obvious, is this: If there are egos involved you have the most control over yours, (once you understand a little bit about how you are reacting and why).

Try to understand why different is not ok with you. If you take the time for a little personal investigation, you will begin to understand your insecurities and how to cope or adjust. You may even be able to re-examine your point of view. As you become more comfortable with who you are and what you believe, there will be less of a necessity to be belligerent, argumentative, and hostile toward those who do not agree.

Remember, if you're not sure what is happening, what you are feeling, and why you are reacting as you do then, "...try to catch, see, understand, and name (label) those emotions that rise so quickly to the surface. Try to understand what you are feeling before everything goes sideways."

BEST CASE SCENARIO

"Different" may become okay and discussed because it supports others, and because that discussion creates an environment that encourages growth, and finds solutions. You may come to understand that others may have either, 1) a compromise, or, 2) the best possible conclusion.

If you can't even begin to do some of that, don't worry. I have suggestions for you in chapters 7, 10, and 11.

Become more comfortable

with who you are,

and less hostile

toward those who

do not agree.

Find a, "Happy Place"!

CHAPTER SEVEN

DIFFERENT MAY JUST MEAN

THAT THERE ARE AT LEAST TWO WAYS

OF DOING THINGS

Different isn't necessarily good or bad. Different may not call for labels or name-calling. In fact, "different", may be an opportunity to honor and value others.

1. Different may mean that two things can be true at the same time.

2. Two ideas can be relevant and have meaning without causing an argument, and the call to cancel one of them out.

3. If we remove the ego from the equation, then most folks will be content with either of two different, good, solutions.

4. The gracious person may allow for the acceptance of someone else's opinion, especially if it is important to that person, or it honors the other person.

5. The acceptance of a different opinion may have nothing to do with the opinion itself. It may be a way of creating harmony and cooperation.

SUMMARY

An open, gracious, conversation is an opportunity to lift someone else up. If circumstances suggest there are two ways of doing things, you then have the opportunity to be humble, extend yourself, set an example, and affirm someone else and their idea. The opportunity to do some relationship building, or keep your mouth shut, may be more important than either idea. In that sense, the idea may not really mean anything at all.

APPLICATION

Who you are, how you respond, and how you handle that moment may be what is important. What type of person do you want to be? Do you care for others? Do you support those around you by affirming them and their ideas?

A PROBLEM WITH APPLICATION

I don't want my look at differences that might not be important, and opinions that could go one way or the other, to detract us from the observation that we are often in disagreement, and we are in significant decay.

IMHO.

Our poor attitudes, bad behaviors, and scarred interpersonal relationships (which are now more likely the norm) add significantly to the seriousness of the situation we find ourselves in. Namely, turmoil in the streets and in homes, dissent, dissatisfaction, division and rebellion, and the breakdown of our republic are problems we all create and share. This question remains: Can we really make any changes?

A PROBLEM WITH YOU TOO

I just re-read the last few chapters and frankly, I don't know how most of you are going to make the adjustment necessary to have the attitude and outlook I describe. Assuming, as we must, that change starts with you.

Some of you have a significant committment to, and dependence on, the woke agenda. You have spent a lot of time and emotional energy barking up that failed and falling tree! Your identity seems fixed and/or stuck.

Can we, "understand our motives, keep ourselves in check, and hold ourselves to a higher standard?" Is it possible for us to, "look out for the interests of others, strive to be gracious, and extend peace instead of resistance and criticism"?

<u>For many of you this book is not suggesting an improvement, it is suggesting a major over-hall, A MONUMENTAL CHANGE,</u>

<u>AND, A REJECTION OF THE WOKE AGENDA!</u>

DO YOU WANT MORE?

I have a few more suggestions as to how individuals change at their very core, but most of that is in another book. That book is, "Victory Over Anxiety Depression and the Human Condition". You can find it on Amazon and elsewhere.

If I included those thoughts here they would be thoughts about the God-given humanity, value, and dignity we all enjoy as God's loved ones. It would be about getting back to who we were intended to be with an understanding that only God can provide. It would be about a change in morality and a transformation in character that a restored relationship with God can make.

It would be about the transformation of individuals.

(And yes, we are trying to do a bit of that transformation here, in this book.)

If you are at a place where you make "no progress", then I suggest counseling, group therapy, and a good hard look at God's promise of transformation, Romans 12:1-2. (And, my book.)

I didn't add these last few paragraphs to discourage you.

I added them to be realistic. I added them to agree with you that a change in perspective, attitude, and character is difficult.

I wrote this book because you can begin to make adjustments. You can begin to change your focus and you can begin to influence others by your improved behavior. As I have stated elsewhere. "You have a great deal of power in any relationship and it is not the power to control, manipulate, or pressure. It is the power you exert when you become someone who listens, someone who is responsible for how they interact, and, someone who cares about others, about harmony, and about constructive dialogue. It is first and foremost the power you have when you set the tone, and set an example."

If your sincere desire is to change and "become a person people don't mind being around, as much as they do now" then there is hope. Admittedly there is work to be done, but there is hope.

ALMOST FORGOT I suggested this at the start of the chapter, "Two ideas can be relevant and have meaning without causing an argument, and the call to cancel one of them out." That's true.

I wanted to emphasize there that tollerance, openness, consideration, and kindness be given to those who see things a bit differently. Support each other. Don't make every conversation problematical,... "choose your battles" ! The best solution's come from a variety of perspectives and different ideas combined together. We don't need to tollerate or cancel ideas so much as we need to gather them together and come to the best possible combined solution.

Do you care for others?

Do you support those around you

by affirming them and their ideas?

CHAPTER EIGHT

DIFFERENT IS NECESSARY

Now, on a lighter note. (After that last chapter I feel obligated to put a positive spin on the "problem".)

Think how boring it would be if everyone was like you and everything was as you desire. Don't take that personally. I don't know you at all. It may actually be great if all of us could implement your ideas, but that won't ever happen.

Since that won't ever happen, that difference has to be okay. Not only does it have to be okay, the concept really is that different and diversity are necessary and needed. Diversity is not only necessary and needed it is, in fact, BEST.

1. We went to Spain not because it was not good here, but because something different was called for. The difference in architecture, lifestyle, scenery, and food was stimulating. (Wasn't crazy about the fried pork belly, and also got a little tired of thinly sliced "Jamon" at every opportunity.) Our mental health improved and our desire for adventure was rekindled, even though I probably gained a few pounds. (Afraid

to look.)

2. You will not always get to decide when or where a different idea or person comes from. They are, or can be seen to be, part of the necessary changes and challenges that life offers. (Keeps us on our toes!)

3. You have no need to change, and thereby improve, if you are alone in your room or in a place where you feel safe. No personal growth occours there.

4. Challenge and change call for introspection, require adaptation, and provide for novel experiences and a greater appreciation of life.

The fun of it all is this; You don't get to always decide when that type of opportunity happens. Remember, we are discussing the observation that most of the difficulty you encounter starts there, somewhere, inside you. **Your greatest struggle is against impatience, prejudice, fear, resistance, and insecurity not against a different idea, a sudden occurrence, new opportunity, or even difficult people.**

The suggestion, to be blunt, is this.

5. Even though an occurance may be difficult, you have a great deal of say in what you learn, how you respond, and how things eventually turn out. The term "eventually" suggests that there may be a fair ammount of work for you to do, and that a positive

outcome may take some time! (That has to be okay too!)

This, is closely related.

6. The satisfaction of a successful struggle only comes when something difficult is overcome. I hated every step of the climb up the hill in Grenada but the fortified Moorish complex and gardens at the top were unbelievable. The difficulty reaching the top of the hill (the work and time) made the entire experience there a little bit more satisfying, although I think I complained at the time.

7. Stimulation, challenge, and even adversity, is a necessary part of life, and in many circumstances it could be said that it gives life meaning. Nothing wrong with having a real sense of victory over adversity once in a while.

8. Challenge and change are better than complacency and stagnation. Not sure what to say here. I guess this statement is agreeable to most everyone.

9. Different is the antidote for boredom. If every sunset was the same, I don't think we would look at them.

10. For that matter, who wants boredom or sameness in a relationship? Believe it or not, you actually want to be married to someone who is

different! Look in the mirror. You really do want to be married to someone else, don't you?

Remember Adam and Eve. She was taken "out of man". I believe that she was similar to Adam in many ways, but she was different enough to be a complementary companion and provide what he was lacking, or Adam would have just gone back to herding his sheep! Eve was different in many respects, and, that was necessary.

Differences, when brought together, complete the whole. These individual differences between spouses, when brought together, make up what is lacking in each individual. Eve arrives on the scene and God immediately sets about suggesting they learn to get along or, "become one".

11. I think we can generalize a bit. A good relationship is only good when each "necessarily" brings what the other is lacking. Every person in a relationship or group is responsible for bringing what they have to that relationship. Everyone has a responsibility to contribute because no one person sees, considers, or understands everything. The emphasis here is on the individual, husband, wife, co-worker and his/her **obligation to bring what they can** to their relationships.

Here again, we see our books stated goal. (We are working on how to accept the difference in our spouses, and in others.)

12. The idea of wholeness and working together is good for a husband-wife organization, or any organization, (no matter the size). Appreciating and incorporating differences is an acceptable and necessary goal for you and your company. <u>The emhasis here is on individuals, groups, or companies that must **learn to welcome others and their ideas.**</u> "Becoming one", or appreciating and incorporating differences, is an acceptable and necessary goal for us all in a varriety of appropriate circumstances and situations.

13. Different is necessary because what exists now doesn't solve the problem. Early painters didn't understand perspective or, at the very least, they had no guidelines and rules as to how to include perspective in their paintings. Someone noticed this deficit and perspective came to be part of the "skill set" that painters used when organizing and crafting a painting.

This understanding and change in the execution of a painting is something we are all forever thankful for. If you don't believe me, just look at a painting that is one dimensional in its' representation of life. It is an unpleasant visual and emotional experience. <u>That is a long way of saying that change is often an improvement, and in that sense, different is necessary.</u>

14. A similar but related idea is this. Different is

necessary because staying the same is harmful. Many people didn't like seat belts but it must be admitted that they are a heck of an idea. If an adjustment makes life easier, more successful, less frustrating, or even safer, then that change is probably for the best.

15. Any relationship, group, or organization that is not interested in change and improvement is not going to meet challenges, make improvements, and grow. <u>Any organization that does not adapt, by considering change, will be left behind. That harms everyone.</u>

16. It is probably true that any relationship needs to, or can, improve with time and change. Something wonderful and refreshing about pushing one another to new heights, experiences, and even different points of view! It is necessary to explore, discover, and find stimulation.

18. Two people might endeavor to go where a person would not think to go, or consider going, alone. You might not consider going to Spain alone but you might consider going to Spain or Sicily with another person or in a group! Yes, we did a group tour of Sicily. I never thought I would get on a bus with a bunch of old people but, it was a great trip. That different type of trip, was really very good. I would not have known that if I had been resistant and not bought the ticket, and given a bus tour a try!

SUMMARY

Something different is often either needed, good, or necessary. An optimistic person knows that it is necessary to look for the good in a situation and they believe that, at least some of the time, change is for the better.

It is necessary to imagine and explore because invention, improvement, novel ideas, and new products come from the freedom to consider how two or more different ideas may come together.

Something different may be absolutely necessary because our welfare and safety, or quality of life, depend on solving a particular problem.

Different may be necessary because it saves the marriage or restores the relationship with the kids. By this, I mean that what you are doing now causes damage and you, of necessity, must do something different.

Something different may cause a small or significant change, and that change can encourage, motivate, bind together, and promote well-being and success on many different levels, both individual, marital, and corporate.

It is also true that something different may be necessary because it gets us off the couch. Challenge, change, and diversity are necessary elements of a life that is lived with meaning and fullness.

Different is an antidote for depression and discouragement. Mental health, success, and fulfillment could be described as embracing a challenge, looking forward to stimulation (new ideas and people), and adapting to change.

The perspective, attitude, and skill-set necessary to find fulfillment includes foresight, optimism, and the ability to understand, deal with, appreciate, and incorporate difference and diversity. It's looking forward to a new experience or seeing things in a new way. It's taking on a challenge to fix or repair something that is broken, something that needs a fresh start. That often includes a new outlook, different strategies, and an effort that includes a fresh sense of purpose.

APPLICATION

If you find change or challenge difficult to cope with then seek to stretch yourself. If you are careful to construct a reality that isolates you and keeps others out, a reality that ensures the greatest safety, then attempt to understand how to overcome your insecurities and fears.

I am not sure it is really possible to stay exactly where you are. It seems to me that you make progress, or you get left behind.

Be fully engaged and:

1. Let those things that cause you concern be things that challenge you, and prompt you to reach out. That, to my way of thinking, is a necessary attitude and a good endeavor.

2. Understand more of what life has to offer. Take on the challenge to include new thoughts and activities, and even new friends. Your mental and emotional health will improve as you consider other points of view, explore new paths, find stimulating things to do, and, as you make new friends. (My wife and I are thinking of taking a cooking class at a junior colledge. I haven't been there for 40 years!)

3. To go straight to the point, many different things are necessary and together they make life worthwhile. If a change in you, and how you view circumstances and those who are different than you, makes life less frustrating, solves problems, makes it more excitinig, or even more peaceful, then that change is necessary and probably for the best.

If you are in a different place, a better place, a few years from now you will have done well. You will have made some of the necessary changes in perspective and attitude.

Isn't it time you learned

how to swim or,

_____ ?

CHAPTER NINE

ADJUSTMENT, HOW MUCH DOES IT TAKE?

How much change might it take? How much effort is necessary?

Both these questions address the concern that the adjustment you need to make might have to be big, or that change might take a long time. Neither may be true. The suggestion, in this chapter, is that a small change sometimes makes a great deal of difference.

1. This suggestion, if it is true, means that only a small change may be necessary in order for you to be successful. (Whatever "successful" means to you.) A quick apology might mend a relationship, ...for example.

2. This may mean that you will not need to expend a great deal of energy making the changes necessary, and/or, that you may see results right away. Would a quick word of encouragement, "do-the-trick"?

3. The suggestion prompts us to ask, what small changes could we make, and what might their effects be? How could you, "tweak", the relationship? How, for instance, would your wife react if you think to take out the garbage without being asked?

4. It may be that you can make significant headway in your particular project or problem by the relatively easy decision to "bite the bullet" and let someone else have their way. In case you didn't get it, I just said that perhaps you need to back off. Don't get in the way. Don't start something. Yes, it may be best that you do nothing at all.

5. Back to the concept of pressure. If you feel inclined to try something that may actually help (make a change), then why not first try a small change in yourself and see what happens next? A small shift in your style or attitude may prompt significant change in others.

(I happened to run across this next illustration, and I'll include it because I like it.)

Small changes do indeed make a great deal of difference. The difference between Estradiol and Testosterone (sex hormones) is very slight. If we drew these molecules on the board most of us would not see any difference between the two. They are two extremely similar molecules, with slight differences that never-the-less, have tremendous effects on the body. The differences in effect are significant, to say the least. They are the difference between male and female, Yes, small changes do indeed make a great deal of difference. (Assumimg, of course, that you think males and females are different!)

SUMMARY

If this book is getting a bit overwhelming, take heart. The changes you need to make may be relatively slight.

<u>As a practical matter, this means that you do not need to worry about changing everything and everyone else. You can concentrate on yourself, as you see fit.</u>

The changes that may be necessary first are the changes you can make in your attitude and perspective. You can make these changes, to the degree that you are willing, in the relative safety and privacy of your heart and mind.

I guess I am saying that you should first consider how you can change because that will be best for you. I don't think that is selfish. Any change in you at all may benefit you and aid in communication, restoration, success, and even in getting your own way, (should that be "necessary").

I don't like using this example because we have had so many fires here in California this year, but, why not try lighting a small fire under yourself, and see if it spreads?

APPLICATION

Is a small change do-able? The answer is, yes. Nothing needs to remain the same. Relationships don't stay the same, they improve or get worse. Taken from chapter 7, "Different is necessary because staying the same is harmful. If an adjustment makes life easier, more successful, less frustrating, or even safer, then that change is probably for the best."

Does your ego (yes, back to that again) permit you to take the first small step? If you managed to make a few small internal changes would you feel better about yourself? How should or could you adjust your style? Do the words you use communicate something unintended? What, or perhaps more to the point, who do you have problems with? Have you considered that there may something you can do about that relationship and that it may be relatively easy to do?

You can make changes. Start with small ones. Remember, you are responsible first for your own attitudes and actions.

Start making a difference.

Go tweak yourself !

I just asked you many questions.

Did you breeze right by them?

Are you afraid to slow down?

What ugly truth might you find if you took a little time?

Here's the deal (I can't beleve I just said that). You bought the book, or a frustrated friend gave it to you, why not do the homework? Pick the smallest "tweek" you can find and make a few changes because different is do-able.

I'll help you do this in the next chapter.

KENT R GORDON

CHAPTER TEN

DIFFERENT IS DO-ABLE

Living and working with those who are different has to be do-able, otherwise, there is no hope. I have made many suggestions. Surely there are one or two that are relevant, ones that you can understand, adopt, and incorporate. If nothing comes to mind, then wait a day or two. Something or someone, who is more different than you would prefer, will come along and you can then begin to apply your new understanding of "difference", and what your options are.

Change is do-able but it takes some introspection and commitment to yourself, your relationships, and your loved ones. We did, in an earlier chapter, discuss the possibility that there are those out there that will be unable to implement any of the fixes described in this book. A change in perspective and attitude will be difficult or impossible for them.

Again, if you are in significant emotional turmoil, if you are really hurting, then be "selfish". Go get the attention you need. Seek counsel and take time to discuss your fears, depression, frustration, and hurt with someone who cares, is skilled, and can help.

YOU CAN MAKE PROGRESS !

Now, to those of you who are motivated to change and able to make a little progress, THIS IS NOT BRAIN SURGERY. Actually, this IS heart and brain surgery. What I meant to say was this. It's not that difficult! YOU CAN make progress!

Go back to a previous chapter that seemed meaningful to you and look again at the questions there. Where do you need to do a little work and what does that chapter suggest? What changes can you make to improve the situation? What small changes in perspective and attitude may be best, or even necessary?

Let me ask those questions again, and in a way that makes them more difficult to ignore.

1. What relationships are difficult and serve no purpose other than to frustrate and block progress?

2. What difficult circumstance or problem has been plaguing you for months?

3. Where is your organization's greatest dysfunction and who or what is the problem?

4. Are you headed for divorce?

5. Who have you offended?

6. Have you made that phone call you know you need to make, or should make?

7. Who is really pissed-off at you? (Vise Versa.)

I suggest these few questions here because these are the types of direct questions that should cause you to take a step backward, be honest, gain insight, and determine what to do next. I believe that with introspection and wisdom, you can find small steps that are do-able.

If you are honest you can find relationships that need some work right now. You can restore relationships, or make those you have more gracious, comfortable, and effective. As you understand where improvement might need to be made, you can make every encounter a little bit better.

Different is do-able and you can get the hang of it one step, or chapter, and/or relationship, at a time.

I looked up synonyms for do-able and found the following: achievable, attainable, feasible, possible, practicable, realizable, viable, workable. Words Related to do-able: practical, reasonable, sensible, contingent, likely, probable, acceptable, believable, conceivable, credible, plausible, thinkable.

One of those words must ring true for you.

A. Can you see that accepting those who are different is practical?

B. Can you see that accepting those who are different is reasonable?

C. Can you see that accepting those who are different is acceptable? ...attainable?

The list didn't mention it, but I might add:

E. Can you see that accepting those who are different is profitable? (Concensus and unity should make for progress in most any difficut circumstance, and in any organization.)

You can feel free to adjust the questions above by inserting words that suggest an attitude you want to gain, or ones that suggest a good pay-off for you.

The suggestion is, the hope is, and it seems to be the case, that if you change everyone around you will react, and improved relationships will be the result. If nothing else, you need to decide what type of person you want to be. As they used to say, "What will be on your tombstone?"

SUMMARY

Successful relationships, bonds of trust, discussions

WOKE RECOVERY HANDBOOK

that increase understanding, and conversations that influence others are possible if you are interested in learning how to understand, and work with, those who are different.

Great relationships are built. They are intentional. As you study and understand BOTH yourself and others, as you embrace diversity of thought and style, and as you consider how best to best to approach each person you come to know, you will create/build relationships that work on a variety of levels.

APPLICATION

That skill-set usually includes flexibility on your part and a willingness to change. Where are your problem areas, and what changes does this book suggest? Most of the application questions in this book are directed at you, your attitude, and how you respond to others. That really is the only place to start.

Are you interested in being a peacemaker and problem solver? Are you going to set an example? Are you willing to compromise for the higher goal of unity, even if it costs you? Are you more interested in giving positive affirmation, than in correction and divisiveness? What label do you wear and should you swap it for a new one?

79

That necessary and needed change might be relatively small, or it might be significant, but it is do-able.

"Just do it, baby!"

CHAPTER ELEVEN

DIFFERENCE CAN GET UGLY

I hope I come up with another chapter because I don't want to end on this one. If you remember the Rodney King incident you will immediately see where I am going. A group of policemen seriously beat an individual, Rodney King.

Many say it was because he was black or "different". I don't really believe that those of you who are interested enough to read this book have a problem with difference or race to the extent that you would do physical harm.

I must, however, ask you what damage you do? The following hard questions will take you to that concern, and please, let me ask the questions a number of ways as perhaps one of them will strike a chord.

1. Does your intolerance do more damage than you think?

2. Do you do psychological harm?

3. Is that damage you inflict long term?

4. Is the situation more serious than you want to admit?

5. Are you in a relationship or marriage that has been difficult for years and years?

6. Have you lost hope because she or he never became the person you wished them to be?

7. Have you created something ugly?

8. Have you cut some people off?

9. Are some relationships beyond repair?

10. Are you suffering the results of your intolerance?

11. Have you lost friends?

12. Are you harboring a grudge?

13. Do you live with feelings of regret regarding the damage you have done?

I am saying that, for some of you, it is possible that your behavior is not acceptable on any level. There is no justification for the way you treat others, the lack of concern you show, and the damage you do. (You probably don't like the way you act either.)

Judgement, hostility, and impatience (among others) are attitudes and feelings that require adjustment. No one wants to be associated with that type of person and no one shoud suffer damage at the hand of another.

I am not going to tell you that you are hostile and dysfunctional. You are going to make that determination yourself, and, you are going to have to decide that enough is enough.

Notice that we are not now talking about slight momentary afflictions, and easy fixes.

YOUR HISTORY

If you are doing damage and you are unable to change or be the person you desire to be, it may be that significant damage has been done to you. Yes, I do mean physical damage, as in abuse etc., but, I also mean psychological damage. History has not been kind to you.

Does your past infringe on and determine your future? Have you been told that the world is an ugly place? Are people not to be trusted? Have you been taught to look for those who would harm you? Are you always careful to protect yourself, or look out for number one? If this is your perspective, then any relationship you form will likely suffer.

If you look at this chapter, or any chapter, and think about a relationship that is a real problem for you, explore your feelings and get stuck, then it is not beyond the realm of possibility that you have been hurt in the past. It may be that you do not have the ability to fashion good relationships because you are angry, withdrawn, sensitive, afraid, compromised, depressed, and poorly taught. Your history has done you harm.

For some reason, I was thinking of damaged and difficult business relationships just above, but, of course, your friends and loved ones suffer with you as well. (I know of marriages that are ear-marked by intolerance, rage, and abuse, rather than compassion.)

All those who know you, either in the home or on the outside, will in one way or another, be "caught-up" in your mess. Everyone suffers the results/consequences of your history, and what you now believe or assume.

REASONS NOT EXCUSES

The observation that you have had poor examples and been mistreated is an acknowledgment that there are reasons for your attitude, and how you perceive the world and those around you.

Your experience to date is NOT TO BE USED as an

excuse, nor is it an indication that things cannot get better. <u>Change is still "do-able" but it may take hard work.</u>

THE PRESENT

You must understand that some of what you have been taught is wrong, and that some of your actions and attitudes are not justified, necessary, and acceptable. The present does need to change, and your history can be understood and set aside.

YOU CAN get the help you need when you are humble, and if you are serious.

You can take steps to make a brighter future but you must first decide that it is time for a change, and in fact, that it is time for a change in you! You must decide that the damage you do is unacceptable. You must decide that those who know you deserve better, and so do you!

You can restore relationships, or, make those you have more gracious, comfortable, and effective.

GETTING HELP TO GO DEEPER

I could say it's time for a little restraint and patience as you "seek to know and understand others", but that is not always exactly right. For some of you the change needs to go deeper. Simply stating that "your history must not be an excuse" may miss the point. The fact that you have been mistreated and poorly taught cannot be, "swept under the rug".

It may be time for a complete restructuring, repaving, removing, or some major "psychic shift" of some kind, (whatever that mean's). Makes no difference what we call it, you may need to understand, and completely reframe, the struggle and difficulty you have and how it is you see yourself and others. You may need an extensive over-hall.

It may be that your deep fears, ideas, and concerns will not be addressed by practicing what this book preaches. There is just too much hidden deep inside you. Many suffer from difficult, personal problems, and you may need help of some kind to help you: 1. Deal with your history and prevoious trauma, 2. understand the hurt you cause, and, 3. decide what a healthy next step would be.

Real damage and emotional pain might require counseling. It may be that your deep hurt can only be uncovered, discussed, and resolved in a therapeutic relationship.

It's very simple, most of us have problems that are hard to solve on our own. If you are this person, it is my opinion that you will first need to take care of yourself. Go find the help you need. Everyone and everything else can wait. Look out for "number one" so you feel better, and so you don't keep doing damage.

If you are really hurting and angry, impatient, critical, etc., then your obligation, as far as I am concerned, is not to struggle and try to apply what this book suggests. <u>Your obligation is to seek out professional help.</u> (Humility is always a good place to start and it might be a great idea for you to get some help.)

That's why "they" invented marriage counselors, therapists, wrote books, and developed resource material.

Pastors, and professionals of many types, are skilled in helping people work through hurt, anger, frustration, etc. Do yourself a favor, find a trusted friend you can open up to, even if it costs you $60 bucks an hour.

This type of understanding, resolve, and effort is the hard work of getting healthy and staying there, and it may take wisdom, insight, counsel, and the encouragement of others to help you get started and help you make progress.

Let's get untangled

The last two or three chapters keep comming back to this question of whether these necessary changes in your character are "do-able". In this chapter, I seemed to return to the suggestion that you may need therputic help and/or the counsel of others. I don't know you, so I am not sure what you need now, or what you can or cannot do.

My thinking is this. I'll just ask you a lot of questions and let you figure out whether you are stuck, broken, resistant, clueless, lazy, etc., etc. You alone can decide who you are, where you are and why, AND, you can decide if you (and others) have probably had enough. You can decide what type of help you need.

I believe most all of you are in one of two places.

A few of you have had an unfortuntate history, and you have habbits and inclinations that are almost impossible to stop. You want to change. Your attitude and your desire's are correct, but you can't get past your history and what you believe now. We have discussed that in different paragraphs and in various chapters, including this one.

You may need the help of others to get started on something new. The problems you need to sort out are not excuses, they are roadblocks that must be looked at, resolved, and removed first before progress can be made.

Most of you "simply" have to decide that you want a different out-look, a new heart, and better relaltionships. Your only impediment is your refusal to admit how poorly you function, how much damage you do, and, that a little humilty and change in you would be best for all concerend. Other than THAT you have no excuses.

I'll probably continue to skip back and forth between these two scenarios. Don't get confused or distracted.

As I said above, most of you just need to get busy doing the hard work you know you need to do. Stop looking for excuses!

Now, to those of you who are not so seriously stuck.

If you recognize yourself and your struggle in one or more of the chapters, then you have real work to do. It may initially be difficult for you, but you can make small adjustments. You don't need therapy, you need to get serious.

If you're; 1. open to suggestion, 2. are listening to your conscience, and 3. are the least bit humble, you can look to see what in you might need adjustment. With a "little effort" you can have the personal satisfaction of making "self-improvements" as you adjust your temperment, perspective, and attitude. A good start may look something like this.

1. You may discover that there are those in your past that need forgiveness. (Hard to hold a grudge and be happy at the same time.) You may have to let that anger and disappointment go. I suggest that your

forgiveness of them is in your best interest.

2. You may need to restore a relationship by <u>apologizing</u> for any role you may have played in the breakdown of that relationship. You can turn the corner and begin to mend relationships that are damaged by taking the first step.

3. Your significant other may be willing to have that <u>conversation</u> that you and they have been avoiding. They may be pleased just to know that you are frustrated, and want to talk and see if things can change!

The first <u>small example</u> you set, at home or away, may be the example you set when you say you want things to get better, even if you don't know how that will happen.

<u>Again, the suggestion is that any small, meaningful, action on your part, will probably be met with cooperation and gratitude. If it isn't, you are not doing it right!</u>

There you go.

Get help or get serious,

but don't stay the same!

INTERMISSION

I am not quite sure I know exactly what an intermission is. Who came up with the idea and what was their intent?

Perhaps the explanation is reatilvely simple. The actors were tired of standing and the audience was tired of sitting. The audience was restless and on the edge of being disruptive. Let's give everyone a break!

Perhaps it was the owner of the theater, or those financially invested in the production. They wanted to sell more poporn and soda so time was made for that.

If a long scene change was needed, then dismissing the audience and giving them something to do (like go the bathroom or find a snack) was wise, timely, and needed.

I think, in hind-sight, that I should have picked a different word. I should have picked "half-time", not intermission. That's a critical time for not only a rest, but for assessment of the game so far, and a time to adjust strattegy for the second half.

Our book so far has been concentrating on relationships. The ones generally thought to be at home or between friends.

Now, in the second half, we will explore the work-place location and look at those relationships more closely.

Folks learn by emphasis, by repetition, and by looking at material/information/insight from different vantage points so this change in emphasis, or vantage point, will not in any way exclude other types of relationships, and the application from here on out should be about the same.

It really shouldn't surprise any of us that the attitudes, skills, and behaviors we are discussing apply to any reltionship. Those at home, and those at work.

Take any example I send your way, from now on, as an opportunity to examine or re-examine who you are and see yourself in different contexts.

CHAPTER TWELVE

STOP, DON'T GO THERE

If you have decided that you want to "get serious", as the end of the last chapter suggested, then I want to introduce this idea of a stop-sign. You can use it as part of your new effort and skill-set.

I want to place a little stop sign in front of you. A sign that says you don't need to go there, you can have compassion. You can view others as "people in process", or "damaged", just as you are. You don't need to go right to "righteous indignation".

Put another way, this chapter is necessary because forgiveness, tolerance, and constructive dialogue (end of the last chapter) are difficult at best. It's much easer to go toward disappointment and criticism. It's easier to blow right past a stop sign and do or say something we later regret.

OTHERS ARE SOMETIMES ALSO DAMAGED

In the last chapter we allowed for the possibility that you were hurt and had a history that taught you the wrong things. I mentioned this in the last chapter, "If you are doing damage and are unable to change or be the person you desire to be, it may be that significant damage had been done to you. Does your past infringe on and determine your future?" "it is not beyond the realm of possibility that you have been hurt in the past. History has not been kind to you."

Yes, you have perhaps been made to be suspicious and cautious. You may be defensive because you were hurt. You may be an angry person, one that has to fight against a short fuse.

I hope you will now struggle to do what is right. I hope you are "getting serious" and working to rid yourself of some of the attitudes and reactions that don't serve you well, BUT:

1. I assume you have not made all the progress you expected to make.

2. I would guess that you are behind schedule.

We all hope that others don't notice our less than noble qualities, or, that when they do notice we kind of expect to be given a bit of a break, or a little forgiveness on some level.

Here are the questions.

1. Shouldn't you be prepared to give that same break/forgiveness/courtesy/ to others?

2. Isn't it possible, and in fact probable, that many of the folks you are having trouble with are hurting, just as you are?

(They may be more damaged than you! If I can say it that way.)

3. What if you accepted the fact that others are afraid, they defend, and they too act out of deep hurt and unresolved conflict?

4. Is it possible for you to take the time to let them know they are heard?

5. How can you support that individual and start a conversation that my be of help?

6. How can you solve their problem, and yours?

7. What if your first reaction was to STOP and wait, then understand or even to console, instead of dismissing and finding fault?

The point of this chapter is this, you must extend the same kindness and forgiveness that you expect to receive, to others. I can assure you that others will

<u>not make all the progress you expected them to make.
They are probably behind schedule too.</u>

If you review the chapters you will see that for every conflict and difficult moment there is an alternative point of view or direction to take, <u>assuming you STOP and take the time to find it!</u>

This compassion, patience, and kindness must be extended to others because that is your only good option.

IT'S YOUR BEST ALTENATIVE BECAUSE: It's is best for all concerned, and it's best for you.

<u>They will feel better, and they will feel better about you.</u>

<u>What could be better than that?</u> (Winning some stupid argument?)

Let me put it this way, ...if we were as hard on ourselves as we are on others, we would be miserable almost all the time. Don't add to another person's misery!

STOP

Remember to stop, take a second, and consider another point of view. Is that person acting out of insecurity, anger, or frustration and resentment? (Even resentment toward you?) It is usually true that even the comment that seems most inappropriate or even argumentative (pushes others away), comes from a person who wants to be heard.

Here, in case you are not getting it, is exactly what to do.

Grow in understanding, before speaking.

I am modeling, in this book and in the various chapters, an important skill-set. It's the skill-set, or inclination, to ask questions and grow in understanding before speaking.

Don't get, "sucked-in" too fast. You can be a peacekeeper, or make any number of interventions that will be truly constructive if you keep youself in check, and first stop to look and see what is happening and why.

If nothing else, it's not that hard to listen and give someone your undivided attention for a moment. Just stop, look, and listen and keep your mouth shut!

I am not exactly sure what "active listening" is, but if it means that you stop and pay attention or listen, then you will not be reacting, talking, and making mistakes yourself. Here is one definition.

"Active listening redirects your focus from what is going on inside of your head to the needs of the person you are talking to"

Seems good to me!

"Shut up and listen", may sound harsh, but it's actually a good idea! The facts are these. Listening and paying attention is often a better intervention than giving advice, correction, or suggestion. Try just sitting there next time and see what happens when you don't enter the fray.

(If nothing else, you won't be one of the idiots in the middle of it all. Whoops, I used a label!)

NONPROFESSIONAL THERAPY

I mentioned the word "intervention" just above. We have all heard about the therapist who "just" sits there as says, "Uh-huh", "Tell me more", or, "How does that make you feel?"

I suggest that there REALLY IS something to nonjudgmental, reflective, active, listening. Take the word Uh-huh, for example. Here is a definition:

"Uh-huh, (used to indicate agreement, confirmation, attentiveness, or general satisfaction)."

IT THAT'S THERAPY, THEN ANYONE CAN DO IT, EVEN YOU!

Can you stop long enough to say "Uh-huh" and indicate that you care. That is so much easier and so much better than "entering the fray".

Use a word that communicates understanding or empathy, instead of all those other words you were going to use that were probably going to indicate impatience or disrespect, and do damage.

REVIEW

My suggestion that you listen and pay attention is meant to suggest that you:

1. Stop.

2. Consider and understand your emotions and reactions.

3. Think about what may be going on in the other person.

4. Think about how it is that others may be hurt so that you do not go over to, "The Dark Side".

5. Think about what might be a reasonable or good goal.

6. Think about what exactly you intend to say or do.

Taking the time to stop, in the discussion above, means that we first take time to do a little internal investigation. That will lead to a better attitude and clear thinking when we next look to see what is happening "out there". It's very simple, if you are squared away (question's 1 and 2) , then thinking of others (3-6) will be a lot easier and more accurate.

ON TOP OF YOUR GAME AT WORK

For some of you, the big relationship challenges come to you at work. Work is where there are so many different types of folks, and there is little room to escape. It is inevitable that there you will meet someone you find hard to understand and work with. There are "others" all over the place!

There will be folks who respond to different types of suggestions, folks who are motivated by different desires and aspirations. Some are very sensitive and must be approached with caution, or at least with insight and concern. Some folks can be relied upon for good discussion, and some for negativity and criticism.

Yes, you have a lot to pay attention to. What is going on in you when you encounter all these folks with various needs?

Some folks, remember, are damaged. Will you kick damaged to the curb, or will you help to mend what is broken? Ask youself that question when you are frustrated, or something or someone doesn't go your way. Use that question to keep yourself in check!

ARE YOU DOING IT WRONG ?

I am not a great "Star Wars" fan, but it does seem to be true that there are forces or powers in the universe. You may wield a bit of power in your little universe. The movie series talks about the struggle we all have with using our power, "the force", correctly.

If you are in middle management you understand who has the power, and who doesn't. (Everyone is answerable to someone else.) When I say, you need to "stop", I mean that some of what you do, and how you treat people, is unacceptable on any level and it must stop.

Add this to your skill-set. Instead of forcing others to act as you would prefer (a misuse of power), let them react to how you are relating to them. People respond (to you) better or more easily than they take orders. Use your power for good, not evil! (More on setting the example ahead.)

MORE ABOUT THE DAILY WORKPLACE CHALLENGE

The wise person, the compassionate person, and yes, the successful person, 1. works to understand himself or herself and, 2. they work to improve as an individual (previous sections) and now, as a part of a marriage, team, or organization they, 3. begin to pay attention to, and understand, others. (this next section)

What's that phrase we used to tell our kids? "Stop, look, and listen."

I want to challenge you to take specific concepts, thoughts, questions, and goals directly into the workplace. Make these (1-7 below) your workplace goals because:

A. There you may find the greatest challenge, and,

B. You will find people who are broken, in need, and struggling.

Stop, or pause on the job, and ask these questions:

1. Am I willing to take time and effort to discover what others want or need, and, how can I help meet that need?

2. What are their feelings or fears?

3. How are they motivated?

4. Are they insecure?

5. How do I include them and make them feel wanted?

6. How do I include them "in the mix". (Feel wanted by others.)

7. What's the best way for me to get my point

across? (If that is even necessary?)

When it gets right down to it, there are a lot of questions to ask and problem's to solve. It's really rather surprising that you have rushed directly to impatience when there is so much work to be done!

STOP DOING DAMAGE

If your search for better productivity, and more cooperation continues by looking ONLY at how others might change and what they need to do, then you are probably making a mistake. An understanding relationship that takes into accout the temprement and needs of the other person is better than coersion every time!

I am saying that if you begin to pay attention to and understand others, then, when you set about changing behavors, responsibilites, or tasks, you will know better how to talk to that specifc person and encourage the needed change.

If you can't do that yet, it may be that you have more work to do first! (That would be in the privacy of your heart and mind, and perhaps, before you even get to the office.) Read chapter four again. That chapter explains how your attitude gets twisted when you concentrate on the wrong things.

If you STOP trying to change others first, and start

to do what I mentioned above and below, your workplace will seem less stressful, more mangeable, and a better place for all.

Here again, is the sequence.

1. You must be first in touch with your desires, what you expect, how you communicate, and how you are prone to react because you will be in so many different circumstances.

2. If when you stop you begin to see the damage you do and the relationships you have harmed, I consider that real progress too.

3. You also must learn all you reasonably can about those you work with. You need to seek to know and understand others and why they are hurt and sensitive too.

4. You need to know what you hope to accomplish. For example: Unity, an improved environment, clarity of task and purpose, good group dynamic's, may all need to be much more important to you than they are now.

5. You need to know how to get others on-board, and bring them along. How to model, and foster cooperation among individuals.

Those three observations suggest this.

A. A significant amount of introspection and

humility, and a concentrated effort to understand and appreciate those who are different, is called for.

B. That effort will enable you to grow in understanding and character, and that, in an of itself, will improve almost any relationship or environment.

C. As you adjust (fix what is broken inside) everything and everyone around you will change too. That is the exciting thing. We are different but we are interconnected. That means you can have an effect on your surroundings, relationships, family, co-workers, and perhaps on your spouse, if you set the right example!

D. Individuals make up the whole, and a whole lot of people can get a great deal done if you know a bit about them, know what you are doing, and if you communicate respect, appreciation, and inclusion.

Do the work this book suggests.

What do you communicate?

What exactly is your "management style"? What might need to change? Can you become the type of person that others want to be around?

Be open and work to gain a new, humble, unbiased perspective. Identify thoughts, feelings AND ACTIONS that are incorrect or misplaced by listening to your conscience and by making observations regarding the reactions you get.

If necessary, seek counsel and bravely discover where your angst, insecurity, and criticism come from. If you don't like what you discover and see, then choose a better alternative by finding out why different is difficult, uncomfortable, threattening, and unacceptable to you.

Make insight, understanding, forgiveness, tolerance, and constructive dialogue part of your bag-of-tricks as you heal your wounds (if necessary) and, as you heal or form better relationships.

Improve your skill-set. Ask questions. Be curious. Don't run a stop sign. What does your conscience say to you right now?

MANAGEMENT SETS THE EXAMPLE

Setting an example is very powerful, and this is why: Setting an example is straight-forward and subtle at the same time!

A good example is obvious (people see it and get it) and, that example gets past any defense or resistance a person might have.

If you set an example (and they follow) they are consciously or unconsciously matching the attitude and "tone" in the room, and they don't have a sense that they are being told what to do.

This again indicates that the change can and must start with you. You set the tone.

(Again, I am tending toward business relationships, but the abillity to go deeper, see clearly, consider options, determine the best course of action and set the example, applies every where, and in any reationship.)

ANY QUESTION IS A GOOD QUESTION

There are many questions throughout this book. A question is a kind of "stop sign". When you ask a question you are supposed to stop, listen, and go deeper (or at least not make a mistake).

Any time you take a second to ask "What is going on here?", "Why am I getting this reaction?", "What's wrong with my friend today?", or any other question that comes from a place of wanting to understand, you are asking a good question.

CAVEAT

Deeper relationships are the most meaningful but it may be that you will not be able to understand your friends or co-workers deepest feelings, and personal struggles. You may not ever really know why they "come across" as they do. In spite of your best efforts, you may gain only partial understanding.

That, of course, leaves us with the options we have been discussing. In a limited sense it is, <u>all about you</u>!

1. Can you change your attitude toward those who disagree, or those who just see things differently?

2. Can you have reasonable success in regulating what you do or say, and how you come across?

3. Can you make yourself understood without prompting anger, frustration, and resistance?

4. Can you change your "style" or how you communicate, so you can improve relationships and be more effective?

5. Can you learn how to have a decent, constructive, conversation with a difficult person?

6. Can you create an environment that encourages openness, is sensitive, and considers other points of view?

7. Can you keep from being, "sucked-in".

8. Can you forgive a person you don't understand?

SUMMARY

Self-control, compassion, empathy, and the ability to step back and view something from another's perspective, are marvelous qualities to aspire to. You need those qualities or graces available in you. They will serve you well with those who are difficult, and for those who stretch you in ways you do not want to go.

You need to be so committed to your task of being the person you want to be that you will not run the stop sign. The stop sign that says, YOU DON'T NEED TO GO THERE!

To repeat. You can view others as "people in process", or "damaged", just as you are. That is best for all concerned, and it's best for you.

If stopping to ask a question keeps you from putting your foot in your mouth, stepping on a toe, adding to the confusion, or raising the level of vitriol, then that brief break, that "stop sign", that question, has already done its job.

A moment of introspection, (What is going on inside of me?), or a moment of observation, (What is going on in this situation or with this person?) is a good thing.

CREATE A CULTURE

What is the best outcome for you and/or your company? The best outcome is an environment that helps to create, support, and maintain cooperative, motivated, individuals. It's a culture where others will reciprocate and make an effort to understand and communicate with each other.

On a more personal note, your best result will be a new collection of associates, colleagues, or even friends that are open and sympathetic to you, your wishes, and your suggestions or proposed program.

All this starts with you. Your compassion and patience with those who are struggling (are damaged), and with those who are just different than you (not so damaged), sets the tone (example).

Extend grace to others.

They are hurting too.

CHAPTER THIRTEEN

THE "HOW-TO" CHAPTERS

I talked a little bit about how to read and apply this book at the end of chapter one. My aim there was to knock-down any defensiveness you brought with you as you started to read. You didn't really know then exactly where the book was headed, and you didn't know whether to trust me and the process so I assume you just read the book to see what it was about. I would guess that you may have not yet done the hard work that real change demands.

Time to go back and do the hard work, the work of introspection that requires humility, honesty, wisdom, and the desire to be "that person".

Let's be honest. We both know that it would be easier to rush to finish this book, than to go back and revisit problem areas, areas glossed over, or areas thought to hard to address and change. That, rush-to-finish, is not a good use of your time, nor is it a good use of this book.

This chapter will help you go back and do the work

we already suggested. The work you avoided. The work that is required to become the person you want to be.

Some of these suggestions can be tried in the privacy of your home and heart. Test them out with little or no danger of being found out.

A few suggestions toward the end of this chapter are things you can try with others. (If what you want to try is helpful, the other folks really won't mind at all. They will, in all likelihood, want to participate, cooperate, and improve their relationship with you.)

ONE PLACE TO RE-START

Which chapter caught your attention, or, which one did you tend to pass by quickly because it was probably true for you, or going to be difficult to do? Look at that chapter again and try to figure out exactly why that different person or circumstance was/is difficult, frustrating, or unacceptable to you. (Use steps 1-13 just below as a guide.)

1. Find a chapter that speaks to you.

2. What is the difficulty discussed in that chapter?

3. How is it that you have the same problem?

4. Go to that place of difficulty and explore your

feelings.

5. Why are you guarded and defensive?

6. What alarms, angers, or frustrates you?

7. What has your attitude been to date? (Feelings are different than attitude.)

8. How have you responded to others and how pleased are you with that response?

9. Can you see where it might be possible and even necessary to view different differently?

10. What, in you, needs to change?

11. What can you do better next time around?

12. Is your difficulty (whatever it is) longstanding, and in-trenched?

13. Is counseling a good option?

Next, in addition to the questions above, read the summary and application for that chapter. Most of the chapters suggest an alternate perspective. Discover suggestions as to how you might adjust your attitude, vision, and response.

Next, if appropriate, think about a specific individual, relationship, or situation that may be aluded to in that chapter. See yourself there. How can you approach that person and change the dynamic?

How can you improve the conversation and that relationship? What could you do differently in that circumstance? What does that chapter suggest?

Why all the questions, (again)?

If you want to think differently, obtain a better attitude, and eventually obtain a better result, then you need to ask yourself the hard, personal, questions:

1. OFTEN,

2. IN DIFFERENT SITUATIONS, AND

3. IN TIMES OF DIFFICULTY.

Change in you REQUIRES REPETITION and you will change more readilly when you learn to ask questions & seek widom <u>both often and in every circumstance</u>. You simply must not react, but stop, look, and listen! Now that you trust me and are making a good-hearted attempt to review "problem areas", I'll ask the hard questions again.

1. What role do you play in your frustrating relationships?

2. Size yourself up. Check how wonderful you pretend to be against the facts and what you know to be true about yourself. (I'll even allow you to put a few labels on yourself it that helps to clarify where exactly your problems are.)

Will this discovery, reflection, and honesty work? Yes. If you take a close look at yourself (go deeper), and look at what's is going on around you (extend yourself), you will find specific areas that need work. With insight, wisdom, and resolve (and new-found trust in the proceess and in me) you can make progress.

GO BACK AND work on your little, personal, dysfunction. If you msised them the first time, I assure you they are still there.

A LITTLE VERY PERSONAL, AND TIMELY, TECHNIQUE

"What exactly is your problem?"

That could be one of the questions you take with you as you go about your business and try to gain insight into others, but I didn't intend it that way quite yet. My suggestion really is that you ask yourself that question and, depending on the answer, that you set safeguards in place.

Yes, you could just ask yourself, "What's my problem?"

Now that you have a little insight, why not make your question more specific? If your problem is impatience, then bring a relevant question with you where ever you go. When you stop, have a good question to ask and answer that helps you with your impatience.

Example, "How am I responding to others and how pleased am I with that response?"

That might be the question you choose to ask yourself when a person or situation frustrates you, and before everything goes sideways. In case you didn't recognise that question, it was #8 in the list of questions a few pages ago.

Asking a good question at the right time not only avoids disaster, but it may help you get to the heart of a problem, (either yours or theirs). That last specific question helps you focus on your problem, and that is probably a good place to start any investigation and decision making process.

The technique, again, is this: Take one of those questions, or any other question that might slow you down a bit, with you as you enter one of your difficult environments, or encounter a difficult person. Ask and answer that question <u>before you make a mistake, ruin a conversation, or say something you will later regret</u>.

What exactly is my problem, seems like a good question to use in most any circumstance (difficult or not), especially if you are asking it because you want to understand yourself and/or others better.

Another general-purpose question would be this:

What am I trying to accomplish here, and is this the best way to do it? (That question should pop-up a lot!)

Are "stop, look, listen",

and "ask question's first",

tool's in your tool box?

KENT R GORDON

CHAPTER FOURTEEN

THE WORK PLACE

In the previous pages we talked about what you should attempt to do, and how you can safeguard against mistakes on your part. I suggested that you can gain understanding and insight regarding who you are, and you can take time to ask questions and understand others.

Old questions return, and new ones appear, in the work place. Problems in your character may show up at work when they don't show up elsewhere. Our group process, our difficulty with others, our new batch of questions (just ahead) , brings us back to the same spot. "If you want to think differently, obtain a better attitude, and eventually obtain a better result, then you need to ask yourself the hard, personal, questions."

What role do you play in your frustrating relationships at work? What is the work place challenge today?

WORKPLACE WOE'S

It's important that we are honest when are talking about the workplace, and this now, is that discussion

We view almost everything first and foremost, as it relates to us and our welfare. We have concerns about how comfortable we are, concerns about how we are coming across, and, concerns regarding what others think about us.

If you had your way, everything would go in a fashion and in a way that makes sense to you, is comfortable for you, meets your expectations, and does not cause too much stress or call for a great deal of adjustment. Everything should go as you deem best.

(If that was true, then you wouldn't have need of so many safeguards, and the need to stop and ask questions would be minimal.)

YOUR DYSFUNCTIONAL GROUP PROCESS

That "everything going your way thing" just ain't going to happen. People are different. They are different than you, and they are different from each other. That means that we cannot fully understand them, or always know what they think about us (usually our chief concern).

We don't, at least initially, know their history and what motivates them, or what their concerns are. We don't know how they are damaged and what they carry around with them (conscioulsy or unconsciously). We can't get all our questions answered.

If we are clueless, or unsure of the motives of others, then we make assumptions about who they are, and what type of person they are. In an attempt to understand, categorize, and manage or control, we label people and put them in boxes. "They are good to work with" or, "They are a problem", "They are critical", "They are not to be trusted".

We can't always or usually anticipate what others might do next.

We all spend time organizing our thoughts, we make assumptions, and we try to get ahead of the situation. We anticipate. We draw conclusions and we set a line in the sand.

All these notions, thoughts, and mental and emotional "activities" tell us more about ourselves than they tell us about others.

We are insecure and we watch out for number one. Many times, we just guess wrong and place barriers where none need to exist.

Of course, there are going to be different people at

the office/meeting. You are going to be there too, and since we just decided we can't figure all of them out, let's start, again, with you.

WHAT IS GOING ON INSIDE OF YOU ?

Yes, back to you again. Let's go deeper and gain some insight regarding you before the day, with others, even starts!

What attitude do you have when you arrive in the office? (That's before any other ingredients/people are added to the mix!)

The "office" includes any place where you are involved with others, <u>and any place your attitude may need adjustment before the day even gets started!</u>

Do you dread that weekly meeting because you know how it usually goes? Are you looking for trouble or anticipating disaster? Do you anticipate a difficult conversation with any particular individual later that day? Are you concerned that your attitude may not be the best, that your frustration and aggravation will show?

Should you have talked to that person before the

meeting? Are you wondering if THIS meeting is the place to have THAT conversation? Are those who may disagree going to meet you halfway, or did you burn all the bridges?

<u>If you aren't in the right head-space **before you arrive**, you know you still have work to do.</u>

(Frankly, if you have that many questions and concerns, and there are many conversation left unsaid, you haven't been trying very hard.)

TOO LATE, the meeting has started! Now what? Pay close attention the next time you are among others in a meeting, or small group of some kind. Do you remember the name of the person you just met? What is going on around you? Are you uncomfortable or, guarded and defensive? If your antenna is up and searching the horizon, is it up looking to see who might be there and whether you need to be extra careful, or avoid that side of the room? Can you relax, or are you working overtime protecting yourself, your ego, and your agenda?

Are you on guard because you know someone will raise an objection, and you know how much difficulty you have with those who disagree? Are you worried that some emotion will rise up in you that makes patience, understanding, and communication difficult? Are you convinced that a drink will help with your nerves, anxiety, and attitude?

Are you concerned that a particular person is at the meeting and that, in your opinion, they will start a problem? Have you labeled them, or others, and put them in a box?

MORE IMPORTANTLY, why has that person, meeting, or type of situation been difficult for you? What buttons do they push? What do these feelings tell you about yourself?

<u>If you aren't in the right head-space **when you are there**, you know you still have work to do.</u>

WHAT CAN A GROUP DO FOR YOU ? (Other than frustrate you.)

It is possible to gain insight when in a group. When in a group you will find additional hints regarding who you really are. Insight and hints you may avoid if left only to yourself. Ones that may not show up any other way.

In a group setting you will have feelings and reactions, and thoughts and concerns, that are unavoidable, and unique to that setting.

I kind of hate to make another list of questions but, as you enter a group, look for clues and hints. Consider the following:

1. Are there little clues (people) here and there that indicate all is not well?

2. Are they reminders that you have some restorative work to do?

3. Are there people in the room, or your chain of command, that you haven't even taken the time to know?

4. Do you see people there that you have written off and dismissed?

5. Are you waiting for him/her to start a problem?

6. Is managing a group process difficullt?

7. Have you done something in the past to gain disrespect?

8. When you experience frustration or anger with that person or in that situation, what are the feelings behind the feelings?

9. Think about it, why are groups intimidating?

10. Could you have managed that person, party, encounter, meeting, or situation better? or,

11. are they all really on another planet?

ENOUGH

I just listed way too many questions, again. No one has all those concerns. No one is that messed-up. I bet, however, that you identified with at least one or two of them, and perhaps more. You may have had many of those feelings and concerns, just not all in the same meeting, or at the same time.

If you decide that you want to have better relationships, change the atmosphere, and be a voice of reason and compassion, then you will need to begin to discover where you need to adjust. As you become less self-absorbed and defensive you will see your mistakes in judgment.

You may still see people who are going to be a "problem", but you will also see them as people who are hurting and in need.

If you view people this way (your choice) then you may develop the skills to manage the problem's that occur from time to time, and set everyone at ease. You can learn to care for many different kinds of folks by watching, paying attention, studying, and learning to see what others need, and what works best for you and others in the group and company.

REMEMBER THE GOAL

Most of the questions I have listed and will list, presupposes you have an interest in being, "that person". Each day, when you're out-and-about, (with others or in a group) you can work on being "that person". Pick an area that "needs improvement" and work on that singular task that day.

You might decide to look to see who needs a word of encouragement. Talk to that person. Be positive.

That's it! You just made a small attempt to be the person you want to be. I can tell, even from where I am sitting, that something changed. The relationship changed, the dynamic shifted, or something else good happened.

A ROOM FULL OF PEOPLE

Don't you want to be "that person" who:

1. is needed at the meeting,

2. is understood to have a positive influence,

3. fosters a good discussion,

4. is known to be even-handed,

5. is respected, even by those who disagree?

That's a tall order but you can be that type of person. Do the work this book suggests.

ANOTHER POSSIBLE PLACE FOR YOU TO START

Start at the beginning. The first few moments are critical in any encounter or conversation. That is one place where "things go sideways so fast". Caution is needed!

When the conversation starts, take a step back, wait and anticipate, seek to understand. Look at what is going on around you (extend yourself). Your radar needs to be up and running, not so you can seek and destroy what comes, but, so you can get off to a better start. Try not to make the same mistakes.

Here again, we are just looking at your attitude, perspective, reactions, and actions. Seek to improve in these specific areas just before, and durring, a conversation.

1. Stop and gather your thoughts/emotions.

2. Anticipate possible problems or objections.

3. Determine to meet those challenges in a

construcive way.

4. Set the example.

5. Raise the level of the conversation.

6. Support the weak or misguided, and,

7. Make sure the insecure feel they are understood.

8. Support others (perhaps even at the expense of what is best for you at the moment).

All those questions are directed at helping you get that conversation off to the the best possible start, BUT, don't forget to ask yourself your safeguard question as well. YOU need to be kept in-check too!

WIN-WIN

The truth is, if you handle the first few minutes of the encounter, discussion, or meeting correctly, you will get off to the best possible start, and you will be appreciated and respected. When you are doing the best for others, you are usually doing what is best for yourself, long term.

What else might YOU double-check or do in a meeting?

1. Maybe you should sit quietly, postpone your agenda, and give your undivided attention to someone else, a recent concern, or a conflict among others.

2. The circumstance's may suggest that now is not the time to provide advice, or emphsise a point, but it is a time to draw others out and let them know you understand and care.

3. Wisdom may suggest that you STOP and take time to understand others so that you can make the best possible suggestion or intervention when that is appropriate.

This verse comes to mind, *"Let each of you look not only to his interest but also to the interests of others"*. Philippians 2:4. The suggestion here is that there is a strong connection between the two, (their interests, and yours).

You must learn to see that your attempt to look out for and understand others, and get the conversation or meeting off to a good start, is the best way to get things done, and incidentally, take care of yourself and your interests. The verse suggests that both happen at the same time.

HITTING THE WALL

We have been introspective (looked in the mirror), and we have looked at how we are with others but things are not always locked-down.

Circumstances, moods, relationships, obligations, and groups change. "Different" may throw us a curve, or "upset the apple cart". Change or challenge may cause us to lose control of the narrative. The conversation may go in a direction that was not anticipated and we may have to adjust on-the-fly. If some of your concerns come to pass, if things "go sideways fast", if you hit the wall, what are your options?

YOUR BEST OPTION IS TO VIEW DIFFERENT, DIFFERENTLY!

Yes, that is still your only good option. I guess you could leave the meeting, transfer out of the department, fire someone, or assign them to a different county, or even a country that is some distance away. Best not to go there.

Go here instead. Think of people, new job assignments, breakdowns, misunderstandings, meetings, and other "unknowns" that invade your space as opportunities to put into practice what I suggest in this book.

THE BIG PICTURE

It may be the case (if it is difficult now and little progress seems to be made) that you should look long-term.

I kind of hate to say it but it may be true that, at

least for a while, the only character change happening is/was change in <u>your</u> character! That wouldn't be so bad, now would it? You get to take that with you where ever you go!

I am suggesting that YOUR new-found wisdom, maturity, grace and the best possible attitude may be the best possible outcome for you, regardless of the difficult circumstances, the less than coooperetive spouse, or the combative work place.

What's the pay-off for that change in your character and attitdue? See 1-4 below.

(The work described is as we have discussed, but the pay-off for you is at the end of each paragraph, and it's a pay-off worthy of the aggravation and effort to get there.)

1. Use your antenna, and the insights in this book, to make yourself, self-aware. What traits, attitudes, or habits, are difficult for you to understand or deal with? Understand the mistakes in judgment you make. Understand how best to approach those you find to be difficult. Don't rush to point out their problem, be quick to understand yours. <u>Be a person who first knows themselves a little better. That will tend to keep your foot out of your mouth, and you may even learn how to say or do something that diffuses the situation and puts the other person at ease.</u>

2. Be a person who sees, understands, then takes the initiative to short-circuit problems. Be a student of your peers. What are they defensive about? What is important to them? How do you best motivate and encourage them? What might improve your relationship with them? Be a person with compassion. Be a person that looks out for the interests of others. Be well-liked and appreciated!

3. Be a person that others listen to because of your insight, humility, reasonableness, and ability to seek the best for everyone. Lead by example, change the culture.

4. As a practical matter, when you are more aware of how you interact, and what others are thinking and feeling, you will communicate better and you will more often get what you want. You can even ask yourself, What, will make me more successful in what it is I am trying to accomplish here with this person, with this particular group, and in this setting? How best do I do that? Learn how to influence others and draw them to your argument by being a person who can discuss instead of polarize. Make things happen without pissing everyone off!

5. Be a person of integrity and character, one who aspires to attain a few of the virtues we discuss in this book. Be a peacemaker. A change in your character is it's own best reward.

BONUS THOUGHT.   <u>You never know who is watching? Others, even the boss, will notice!</u>

SUMMARY

It would be fantastic, and probably a good career/ life move, if you could maintain a good attitude, make the best decision, and provide the best counsel when things are not the best. What if you were the "best person for the job" when "things get ugly"?

The wise person, the compassionate person, and yes, the successful person, works to understand himself or herself, and they work to improve. They also work to understand others both as individuals, and as parts of a marriage, family, team, grouip, or organization.

The best outcome, of course, is that others will reciprocate and make an effort to understand and communicate with you.

Your best result will be a new collection of associates, colleagues, or even friends, that are open and sympathetic to you, your wishes, and your suggestions or proposed program.

Your character

will be appreciated

by someone eventually,

(if not sooner)!

CHAPTER FIFTEEN

OPTION THREE, EVERYONE TOGETHER

YOU FIRST BY YOURSELF

"Going deeper" is first and foremost an inward, and perhaps, a deeply personal matter. In the previous pages, we looked at what insight you might gain, and what changes you might make, after looking in the mirror. I have suggested that you think about yourself and how you have been acting or responding. What is difficult for you?

YOU WITH OTHERS

I also suggested that you pay attention when you are in a meeting. How and why do "they" bother you? How can you view those people differently? What are their needs? We discussed what you might learn when you pay attention to the first few moments in an encounter/conversation/meeting. What do you see? What is your perspective? Are you in touch with your feelings, reactions, and actions? What should you be doing and thinking when you enter the room?

<u>There may be a third option.</u>

EVERYONE TOGETHER

Is a group effort possible? (For our purposes here, a group is two or more.)

A VERY SMALL GROUP EFFORT

If an interpersonal difficulty is relatively slight, and you want a better relationship, then talk to the person you are having difficulty with. If you are sincere in your desire to mend or improve a relationship you will do well in this conversation.

Ask them what they see. How do they think the problem can be resolved, and the relationship improved? If you determine to ask these types of questions, then you must be ready for what you might consider to be criticism.

If you ask a risky question and press for an immediate answer, the conversation may not go smoothly. If it doesn't go well there is probably "blame" to go around. You may have asked the wrong question or asked it poorly, or you asked the right question at the wrong time.

It's probably a good idea to suggest that a difficult conversation takes place at a later point in time. That allows the other person to do a little introspection and figure out how they want to say what's on their mind. They may want a little time to figure out how to have a decent conversation, and not be too rough on you.

A LARGER GROUP EFFORT

If you have the guts, why not ask a few of your friends or employees to give you feedback. If you are really brave, give "the group" a few questions to answer. (Even asking a question sets a new tone.)

Here are a few possible questions:

1. How was your service today?

2. Did the meal arrive promptly?

3. Were the options explained to you with patience and sensitivity?

4. Did I listen to you and allow you to express your

concerns?

5. Are you getting the help you require?

6. How has your time here been?

7. Can you suggest a small change we might consider

making?

8, What could we do to take unnecessary stress away?

9. What frustrates you about this job, your role, or

what you are asked to do?

10. What process or procedure could we cut or adjust?

11. Where do we lack communication and how could that be improved?

12. Is there something you have wanted to say to me, or ask of me?

Or course, if you're not running a restaurant, some of those questions would not apply. If you're paying attention at all to what's going on around you, questions should come easily to mind, ones that fit your situation and apply to your relationships, and/ or, personnel. You should know where some of the problems are (where the skeletons are buried) before you ask!

YOU CAN BRING THE GROUP ALONG

It may be that you want to improve relationships, promote discussion, encourage creativity, or even change the culture. You can find a way to guide your group/staff through a discussion that indicates to them that you want improvement or change. You want what is best for them and the organization. I guess I am suggesting some sort of "group process".

If you can't see yourself asking the questions above, or asking other specific questions, you can start a focus group, or provide a hand-out. If you are in business there are many books, pamphlets, workbooks, questionnaires, or instructional materials already in use and available to you.

Find a resource that will help you and your company improve the culture, foster the exchange of ideas, promote harmony, and, go the direction it needs to go.

If you have big bucks or discretionary spending, then you can go on fancy retreats like my wife's company did! Now back to reality. "Reality" being the fact that you probably aren't going to get five thousand dollars to take 7 or 8 people on a retreat.

The types of products and materials I mentioned above are possible to find and purchase at a reasonable cost. It is possible to start a focus group on-site. That doesn't cost a dime.

If nothing else, you can begin to model the type of behavior and communication you expect from others. It doesn't necessarily take an intervention or group pow-wow, just ask a few questions. Show others that you are concerned about them. That is very powerful too.

START NOW

Retreats or focus groups, small casual discussions, or, one on one, the reality is, that with your leadership, the necessary changes can be made.

OF COURSE, DUHH!

As I write or rewrite, I try to edit and keep my focus clear. I noticed that this chapter swings back and forth between the individual and smaller interpersonal problems, and, group or corporate concerns. Of course the thoughts swing back and forth. A corporation is a group of individuals. The two concerns are inter-related.

This connection suggests two observations that, at first glance, seem in opposition to each other.

1. The first observation is that each individual must feel supported, and they must feel their efforts are appreciated and valued. That's very personal, and that type of care and support is accomplished best in one on one conversations. That type of support doesn't "automatically happen" as part of some big group dynamic. That kind of encouragement falls on you to provide.

2. The other observation is that an employee must feel to be an important part of something larger. They must feel connected to others and a larger goal. A feeling of isolation, of being disconnected, is discouraging and it does not create a culture of cooperation, support, empowerment, and creativity.

THE SOLUTION

A decent boss is self-aware, open-minded, and skilled in both interpersonal interactions, and large-group relationship building.

You can determine to, and learn how to, encourage others to talk with you and to each other if and when you decide that is important.

<u>When you value a person and their contribution in front of others, they will value them too.</u> You can intentionally and actively let someone, in a group meeting, know they are valued. YOU can tell them so, and, as more people observe and are included in this type of positive feedback, they are connected to each other and the whole. They might learn to encourage each other!

This positive "group process" creates a good environment that solves both problems (lack of support for an individual, and isolation from others).

Your best outcome is that your particular group will come to trust in, and encourage, each other. Now, go show them how!

A group is only as good as the sum of its parts. Or, "Ingredients are not good or bad in and of themselves, but understanding them and putting them together properly makes all the difference in the world. Ingredients, who come together and cooperate, make for a nice cake."

THIS MIGHT ALSO BE A GOAL FOR YOU, YOUR GROUP, OR ORGANIZATION

When we say that it is necessary to "understand the importance of difference" in the group/work environment, we are saying that:

1. The program must be sensitive to what works best for both the individual and the group or company.

2. The structure must accommodate, or make room for, those who tend to see things differently.

3. It must seek to listen to those who have something else, or more, to say.

4. The culture should encourage discussion, openness, and cooperation.

5. Management must model discussion that promotes inclusion and supports individuals.

6. There must be a "mechanism" in place where grievances can be noted.

7. Any person with an attitude that is critical or divisive must be taken aside, in private, and allowed to express themselves.

8. A critical atmosphere in the work place must be discussed first with managers, then with individuals, then, if necessary, in a larger context. (A group discussion)

9. Management must understand that, "A corporation is a group of individuals. The two are inter-related."

10. Different expressions, concepts, ideas, and personalities come together to make a whole.

11. Difference is the other "mother of invention", and difference makes life, and work, an interesting challenge.

12. Invention and progress, by definition, are different than what went before.

13. "Success" takes many different individuals, with different personalities and skill set's.

It has been said that something that is "whole" is complete and lacking in nothing. I listed those questions because your company might be lacking in one or more areas.

I don't know that I got those observations in the correct order. The one that stands out to you, the one that is missing in your workplace, is the one that you need to work on.

Let your company work hard to understand what works best for each individual and for the company as a whole. **THIS MEANS THAT YOU** must be be brave and dilligent and look for any individual or sub-set that may need help, or ask any question necessary in order to help shed light and show you where improvement is needed.

Be a company that embraces different individuals

and let them enrich the environment, and the day-to-day work experience. Diversity of style, thought, emphasis, concept, and personality makes for a "technicolor life" and for a productive workplace (where everyone is valued).

"Something different is often either needed, good, or necessary." (Different is Necessary, Chapter 8.)

That's a good goal for a company.

YOU'RE ASKING A LOT

Even with the best of intentions most of us move slowly toward our goals to improve. The facts are that when we see a relationship flourish, or see improvement in one direction, another person will arrive on the scene that either challenges what we have learned, what we have set up, and/or asks us to try harder.

Thankfully, I have a way to look at this problem of never getting it all figured out, and the continuing problem that certain types of people (different people) keep popping up here and there.

These first thought's occured to me.

1. It's a "natural law" that opportunities for growth just keep popping up. It's like "Whack-A-Mole". One relationship is on the mend, then another person that is a bit of a challenge pops up and we start all over again. More questions arise. What can I do to resolve this new conflict? How do I react to this person? Why about them bothers me? How do I change the environment or diffuse this situation? How did I get caught off-guard again? All good questions.

2. We are tested and there is always room for a little introspection, improvement, and personal growth. That opportunity to understand, stretch, grow, and improve (if embraced) is a good thing.

SUMMARY or BACK WHERE WE STARTED

All these different relationships and the challenges they bring make life, and work-life, interesting.

1. Try to see differences of thought, skill, attitude, temperament, and motivation, as part of that diverse place we call "the office", or even our home.

2. Be a person who is appreciated and respected when he/she walks through a door. (Makes no difference what or where that door is.)

3. Embrace individuality and difference and, if you get far enough (are mature), you can love, empathize,

encourage, and be a person that sets the right example.

4. Endeavor to be, "that person".

I wish you success. Decide if the goal of a restored relationship, an improved work environment, or a marriage that is on the mend, is a goal worth pursuing, then get to work on yourself first.

Take an entirely new character

with you,

where ever you go!

(The group, the group process,

the conversation, the company,

and the home,

will be better for it!)

AFTERWORD

I am going to tell you why I wrote this book. I know that this information is usually included in the first few pages, or in the preface or foreword, but I thought it best to leave politics to the end as they are so divisive. (If I started off talking politics, I would have made a tactical mistake.)

Politics, our nation's present circumstances and climate, and the rampant wokeness and the estrangement we see among and between individuals, concerns me. That concern prompted me to ask why we have such a problem with those who are "different"? As Rodney King said, "Can't we all just get along?"

I see immorality and intolerance displayed on the news every night and it frightens me. It makes me wonder if the politicians ever turn on the evening news and see how they come across? (If I noticed that I acted like a buffoon in front of others, I probably would not take the podium again until I had apologized and cleaned up my act. I certainly would not want my grandkids watching.)

Those who are different are categorized as sexist, racist, radical right (or left), as homophobic or intolerant. A nation cannot stand if it is at war with itself. Our dirty little snowball is going downhill fast, and, it keeps rolling and picking up size and momentum. If not turned around soon, our destruction will be great and wide-spread!

Everyone, regardless of affiliation, ethnicity, sex, or political bent has work to do of some kind. The work and adjustment that needs to be done first are done in the heart and mind of the individual.

That is why this book did not need to start with an inept discussion of all the possible political solutions to political and social unrest. I didn't go there. (Be sure to know that some write extensively on the nature of our political system, and they have greater insight into our history than I. Not sure they have any answers however.)

I have just enough information and wisdom stored away to talk with you about the possibility that you might raise yourself above the fray, and become a force for restoration, understanding, and compassion.

I have laid out a few thoughts as to what type of work you might need to do, how you might be stuck, and the adjustment in mind and heart you should consider.

These frightful concerns regarding who we seem to be, or are becoming, is what prompted me to write this book! I didn't write down all my thoughts about these diverse concerns (political and otherwise) for you, because you can't do much about them. Your job, your obligation, your best options, is to work on yourself. . (I secretly hope a few politicians will pick this book up and read it too.)

My area of interest and subject matter revolves around a basic concern. My singular concern, and yours too, must initially be, what type of individual do I want to be, and how do I want to be seen by others?

Every individual has the opportunity and obligation to listen, empathize, heal wounds, and restore relationships. Everyone has that monumental task.

Politician, woke-warrior, frustrated and angry or not, ask yourself these questions. Can I be trusted? Can I be tolerant? Can I be sensitive to those who disagree? Can I make my point without resorting to name-calling, and hate? Can I have a conversation and get my point across without offending and bringing the discussion to a halt?

What tactic, lie, or misrepresentation am I willing to put aside? Can I put aside labels or identity politics? Am I more interested in honesty than manipulation? Are solutions more important than grandstanding? Can I form relationships and bonds that are constructive?

Can I work across the aisle? Do I understand that I am morally and legally obligated to represent the majority and not those who are loudest, or have the most to put in my re-election campaign bucket?

Can the three different branches of government work together to make us whole again? Can I represent my constituents when I would rather bow to the radical element, or those who might have the resources to re-elect me?

Is getting a vote or retaining power worthwhile if the nation is broken, at odds, has no hope for the future, or lacks trust in its leadership?

"A hostile nation makes no progress and loses its humanity."

"Woke" accomplishes next to nothing. Battles for power are divisive. Pushing a false narrative, encouraging dis-content, and fanning the fires of identity politics creates disunity and destroys nations.

Questions regarding the health of our nation are questions of personal integrity, kindness, tolerance, and responsibility. Our relationships, whether interpersonal, corporate, or political, are directed and determined first by who we are, by our character, and by our morality.

We are a nation of individuals and, as far as I know, the place to start the revival we need as a nation is in the hearts and minds of the individual. The only phrase that comes to me at the moment is, "What does it profit a man if he gains the whole world but loses his soul?" (Mark 8:36) Have you lost your soul? If your soul is lost or is in significant disrepair, you just don't need to be managing my world.

(That's as political as I am going to get.)

FINAL THOUGHTS

The best place to start, and end, a discussion regarding the need for a new perspective or a change, is discovering, discussing, and understanding that place in ourselves that needs adjustment.

Our difficulty with difference bring us to our knees as we come to understand that we are not who we wish to be. We are often prone to be defensive, judgmental, and critical.

As you understand yourself, your prejudices, your insecurities, what motivates you, and what threatens you, you can better understand how to regulate your feelings and reactions, and your tendency to find fault and criticize.

As you become self-aware and make a few adjustments in perspective and attitude, it may perhaps become ok with you that others express themselves, and have an opinion of their own. You may find it to be just fine that others are not the same as you.

If you model the behavior you would like to receive,

you may meet less resistance in return. If you are gracious, patient, and tolerant, you might find that you are allowed to express your opinion. You may learn how to have a conversation with others that is constructive and finds solutions.

You may eventually understand and be comfortable with this, "Being different must be okay and if properly understood it is a welcome part of our technicolor life."

That's maturity. That's wisdom.

You can create a change in the relationship, marriage, group, or workplace but this won't happen until you look at yourself and understand:

1. What you communicate (intended or not),

2. How you interact (interpersonal skills),

3. What your attitude and temperament reflect (who you are at your core), and,

4. How you deal with diversity and difference (how skilled you are at practicing what you preach).

I believe that, if you have been the least bit honest as you read this book, there are people who have come to mind. They may have come to mind because they are a real pain, or they cause you difficulty of some kind.

Others have come to mind because you know you

have been less than kind. Look closely at difficult relationships, even those that you assume are beyond repair. Step back and consider how you might have it wrong? Is that situation as bad as you surmise, and can in be fixed first by an adjustment on your part?

It makes no difference how the relationship came to be in disrepair as now you have some insight and some of the tools necessary to heal wounds, reconnect, and save friendships.

Go to someone this week and own your part in that difficult relationship. Decide today to seek out that person you have cut off. Determine to talk to that person you have harmed. Decide to reconnect, and even apologize, if necessary.

Are you, with at least a small amount of humility, willing to start a long-overdue conversation? This is Important. If you start a conversation with a person you have had difficulty with in the past, 1. be sure you know where you want the conversation to go, 2. know what you are trying to accomplish in this initial chat, 3. make sure to keep yourself in check, and 4. be sure to stop if it goes a direction that is not constructive, or it reinforces previous hurts.

Be introspective. Go deeper and make a few, very personal, adjustments, AND seek to understand those who are different because, "different happens".

Then, like Superman, "Save the Day", or at least get

out there and see what small changes you can make, (being mindful of who you want to be, and what you want to accomplish).

Remember this? "You went to war with the wrong attitude, the wrong weapons, and with the wrong strategy. You fought a fight that was doomed to be lost before it started."

Now, you know better.

Be gracious, tolerant, constructive, and supportive. See and enjoy what happens next! You will feel better about yourself, and others will feel better about you.

"Become someone people don't mind being around,

as much as they do now!"

Printed in Dunstable, United Kingdom

70572933R00092